The View from Here

JOAN BAKEWELL

The View from Here

LIFE AT SEVENTY

theguardian

ATLANTIC BOOKS

LONDON

First published in 2006 in Great Britain by Atlantic Books on behalf of
Guardian Newspapers Ltd. Atlantic Books is an imprint of Grove Atlantic Ltd.

The Guardian is a registered trademark of the Guardian Media Group Plc.
Guardian Books is an imprint of Guardian Newspapers Ltd.

The author and publisher would like to thank Faber and Faber Ltd
for permission to quote from copyrighted material: 'The Love Song of
J. Alfred Prufock' in *Selected Poems* by T. S. Eliot © 2002.

ISBN 1 84354 514 4

A CIP catalogue record for this book is available from the British Library.

9 8 7 6 5 4 3 2

Designed by Nicky Barneby @ Barneby Ltd
Set in 12.25/16.5pt Monotype Garamond
Printed in Great Britain

Atlantic Books
An imprint of Grove Atlantic, Inc.
Ormond House
26–27 Boswell Street
London
WC1N 3JZ

Contents

Introduction

EACH OF THE LANDMARK DECADES in life offers a frisson. Our culture operates by numbers and 'the big O' offers a chance for a larger than usual party as well as for a little introspection. But the approach of seventy seemed, for me, more laden with significance than any other birthday had been. It gave a public label to something I didn't feel: being old. Rather than let it slip by, I thought I would do something to mark a new departure in my life. So I began a column for the *Guardian* newspaper called 'Just Seventy', a title named in gentle mockery of the teenage magazine, *Just Seventeen*, now defunct, as is the *Guardian* column.

The effect was exactly as I had hoped. I felt a renewed sense of purpose about life, a sense that I still belonged to the community of journalists among whom I had worked for many decades, and also that I had a role that connected me, on a broader level, to other people.

These are things that tend to fall away as you get older. A sense of purpose that drives the young and directs the mature seems no longer needed in later years. The effect is to leave you stranded high and dry, out of the mainstream of ideas and activities that animate the working population. It takes real effort to reconfigure your life to stay within that community. Being a freelance as a journalist and a broadcaster is to be free of the daily constraints of consistent, unvarying employment. That, given the Byzantine managerial intricacies of today's media operations, is often a blessing. There is to be no sudden lurch at retirement from diary-heavy commitments to wandering aimlessly around the house. But on the whole society still believes that the old should have better things to do than insist on being as active as they ever were. Although, under pressure from the pensions crisis, a move is now afoot to keep the population working longer, there is no genuine consideration given to how people's later working lives might be made a source of fulfilment and satisfaction. Given our longer life expectancy and falling pension pay-outs, how this can be done needs to be positively addressed. My limited experience so far tells me that involvement with other people is a major pleasure that the old take in life. Its converse is the isolation and loneliness that afflicts so many.

This is, after all, merely the third of the three ages of man. Its span is as great if not greater than the earlier two. The distance from sixty to ninety is as far as from twenty to fifty, a fact that the old, their behaviour and their attitudes sets in perspective. That's why this book doesn't make such generalizations. It is not about issues; it is not a how-to book of advice and homely wisdom. It is rather a personal record of how I feel about being over seventy, based on and augmenting those *Guardian* columns. The responses to my e-mail address printed at the end of each column show that I struck a chord. Many people wrote to me of their own lives, added to my arguments, corrected my mistaken memories and took up many of the points I wanted to raise. I liked that. It convinced me that there is a huge communality of interest out there in society that remains somehow untapped and unappreciated. I look forward to the day when the old are not referred to as 'them', a problem to solve, but as 'us' at the heart of an active and lively community. I hope this book does something to bring that time forward.

PART ONE

Today

'For age is opportunity no less
Than youth itself, though in another dress,
And as the evening twilight fades away
The sky is filled with stars, invisible by day.'

HENRY WADSWORTH LONGFELLOW

ONE

A Place Called 'Old'

PREPARE TO BE OLD, to be very, very old. Projections made early in 2006 promise that many more of us will live to be a hundred. Some ten thousand do so already; indeed, the question arises of whether, twenty years hence, the Queen will be sending herself a congratulatory card. The number of centenarians could increase tenfold in the next sixty-eight years. By 2074 there could be 1.2 million people over one hundred. According to that admittedly speculative calculation anyone now in their thirties has a one in eight chance of reaching that age. So how do we view the prospect? I have in recent years hit the problem head on, writing about my own age and ageing in regular articles that to my delight have prompted an enthusiastic response, proof if it were needed that the old are still engaged in ideas and eager to exchange them. This book collects and extends some of those ideas, giving them a more recent perspective and adding others that have occurred to me. Each day seems to bring new experiences and insights that are just not available to those who haven't travelled this far in life.

To most people old age is a bad smell, a nasty place of bedpans and stair lifts, of bleak care homes and nurses who call you 'love' and 'dear' simply because to them all old people are alike. The public image of age is grim too, reinforcing a cosy contempt: too much 'grumpy, old' this and that, and songs that ask, 'Will you still love me when I'm sixty-four?' while expecting the answer 'no' of course. Headlines that harp on pensions, euthanasia and neglect may be justified but they aren't the whole story. I know plenty of old people living feisty and fulfilling lives. My oldest friend, aged ninety-four, is currently enjoying the writing of Gabriel García Márquez and no, she isn't a graduate or a middle-class professional. She's simply a very intelligent woman whose humdrum life hasn't inhibited the use of her wits. I like to think there are many like her; it's a condition I aspire to in the coming decades.

We need, each and every one of us, an entirely new attitude to being old. It is, after all, the destination we deliberately set out for, the result of all those diets and exercise crazes, the purpose of the acres of health advice and food labelling. It's the natural outcome of flu jabs and health and safety inspections. What was it all for if not to live longer and remain fit? We are living in a far healthier world, a cleaner environment than in my grandmother's day. At the turn of the twentieth century the average life expectancy for a man was forty-five and for a woman forty-eight. How far we have come is nothing short of miraculous. Science has helped and is going on helping; stem cell technology is now at the threshold of developing body part replacements than can keep us regularly repaired. Body MOTs are not out of the question. We are living through a quiet revolution that is transforming the trajectory of our lives.

And in old age we are reaping the fruits: not a sudden lurch into a smelly decline, but vistas of years ahead of modest pleasures; horizons that are no longer set by the needs of family, the career ambitions, the immediate and intense business of daily survival. Hip replacements, cataract operations, heart pace-makers are rendering us active, even spry. As someone in the lower foothills of old age, I can bear witness to the abundance of energy and enthusiasm waiting to be used by people in their sixties and seventies. The University of the Third Age flourishes. The Open University is full of oldies. Literary festivals throughout the summer are thronged with grey-heads keen to know and question, learn and debate. 'Learning for life', a government slogan, now extends well after retirement. In their leisure time, the old aren't just boozing and cruising: the hardier spirits are climbing mountains, visiting the Pole, meeting sponsored challenges. I have a friend in his late seventies who has recently taken up tap-dancing. How's that for bravura!

People in power who now decide how we live need to be more aware of how the culture is shifting. As more live longer the changes can only accelerate. Even the young need to look beyond the stereotypes. *Little Britain* may be funny but it's sometimes also insulting. 'Old' is not another country, a place you're shunted off to when the real business of life is done, where you're parked in the ante-room of death and live in expectation of its imminent arrival. It is an era, as vividly a part of living as any other. It may be situated at the other extreme from youth but being old is not being ill. Life can be as full of value and delight, of incident and insight, as it is for a twenty-year-old. And now every twenty-year-old is likely to arrive there eventually.

The sudden watershed of retirement will have to be modified. There must be more varied and adaptable options than simply working full tilt until sixty, then slamming the door on all your wisdom and experience. We shall all certainly have to work longer. The whole economic house of cards will collapse unless we do. But that doesn't mean we have to stay in the rat race, with the stress and competitive thrust that gives middle age its ulcers. We need to plan for part-time, less hectic working lives, in jobs that society needs and welcomes, yet in which we also feel needed and valued.

The numbers of friends and contemporaries will thin out as the years go by. Death takes its toll in the face of even the most optimistic statistics. So we will need to stay close and grow closer. Families, local friends and neighbours will take the place of business colleagues and working contacts in their daily import-ance. At the same time, old friends across the globe can now be in touch via the internet. I have had more contact with old school chums in the last ten years than in any earlier decade. Yet it is also a time for the different generations to get to know each other. The existence of those apparent barriers that keep them apart – text jargon, say, or crazy clothes – can't be denied, but the two sides can be teased into some mutual respect. And the dangers of depression and stoic resignation that plague the lonely can't be ignored. I'm not saying old age is a bed of roses. But now we're all going there, let's fix it so we enjoy the journey.

~

THINGS WERE SO DIFFERENT IN my grandmother's day. She was born in the 1870s and when she had her seventieth birthday in 1947 I wrote a poem in honour of her great age. I was a gym-slipped schoolgirl at the time, much in love with Tennyson and Browning, and the embarrassing lines of my rhyme bear the unhappy traces of their influence. I speak of the 'flame of youth' – that's what she'd lost, and 'life's dwindling rays' – that's all she had left. The whole was written out in faultless copperplate, lending dignity to its callow sentiments. The tone was elegiac, giving thanks for a life dutifully spent and now nearing its end. It wasn't; she would live to be eighty-six, but to a child she seemed ancient at seventy, a stooped, white-haired figure crippled by rheumatoid arthritis, walking with two sticks.

Years roll by and it was recently my turn to hit threescore years and ten. Seventy: an ominous number by any reckoning, but nowhere near as bleak as in my grandmother's day. In my turn I duly received a clutch of spirited home-made cards from my grandchildren, admittedly younger than my pious thirteen-year-old self. No copperplate now, no tone of slightly fearful respect. Instead my greetings – conflating the graphic freedoms of artists Cy Twombly and Bridget Riley – were an uninhibited riot of colour, with the casually expressed wish, by one of them, that I should 'have a good day at the beach'. As indeed I did. How times have changed.

Seventy years: landmarks don't come any heavier than this. We giggled at thirty, with mock angst at saying goodbye to youth, but sharply aware that we were coming into our prime. At forty we glowed with busy lives going well or frowned with doubts as the options narrowed; we called it early middle age. We preened at fifty with some things well done and mistakes made and buried; we laughed at sixty in the warmth of a lifetime's circle of friends. Those of us who go through life keeping in touch, never quite leaving behind each era, probably had the greater reach. But most of us have that close-knit group of around a dozen or so whom we keep close. And surely this was still late middle age. But at seventy there's no denying that even by the most generous reckoning, it's the beginning of getting old. And note how even now I'm pretending it's merely the antechamber to age.

For the ominous day itself, I tried going into denial. I tried to pretend it wasn't happening. No party this time round. Instead, I fled the country. I went to France for a week with the immediate family, disguising it as little more than an Easter holiday. Easter – a moveable feast – has always been entwined, via ancient calendars and phases of the moon, with my actual birth date. Jesus may have returned to earth from the dead on Easter Day, but it was on Easter Day that I first arrived. What's more, I was christened at Pentecost, so I feel that the Church's celebrations have me in their shifting grasp.

Here I am reaching that age so particularly marked in the Old Testament, with its resounding threescore years and ten. But there's hope within its pages too. It's here that Methuselah lived to be 969 years, fathering his son Lamech when he was 187. His father Enoch lived to be 365 and his grandson Noah 950. All of their forebears lived for between 895 and 962 years, filling the gaps needed to trace the line of Joseph, Jesus's father, back to Adam and hence God, who is older than time itself. Quite what religious fundamentalists who believe in the literal truth of the Bible make of these statistics I don't know. But perhaps they show that even in Judaic times when mortality rates were low – what with famines and plagues and such – certain people lived to a great age, though none of them appears to have been female. So not much comfort there.

Today we have bright modern statistics of our own. In the developed world, life expectancy has been increasing steadily since the 1840s. Currently women are living longest in Japan, on average until they reach the age of 84.6; France is nearly as good with 82.4. In Britain life expectancy for a woman is 79.9. Because I've survived thus far, my own is something more than that, though not by much. Not surprisingly, for me these figures have ceased to be mere statistics. At what point, I wonder, do I begin to reckon on just ten more springtimes, ten more Christmasses? Can I, medical prognoses being what they are, estimate the ages my grandchildren will be when I reach the final shore? That way I can scare myself silly into, you might say, an early grave. But it's no way to have a life. After all, at the age of eighty-five my father bought a brand-new car, giving up his ageing Rover for a foreign model. He was of a generation who, ever since the war, had refused to buy either a Japanese or a German car. 'I don't forget what they did to Ernie Edge in that prison camp,' he would explain. Now here he was, finally moving on and conceding that world trade had superseded even the most legitimate grudge. He also regularly played nine holes of golf a day, skirting the other nine, to meet up with friends at the reassuring nineteenth. His mix of healthy exercising and cheerful socializing seems to me an excellent way to live. I hope I have inherited his optimism. Perhaps there's something in my psyche that is editing out the future finality, and leaving me no older than I feel.

Certainly, at the age of ninety-six, the Brazilian architect Oscar Niemeyer created a wonderfully designed pavilion for London's Serpentine Gallery. In the same week in 2003 the then Tory Chairman Theresa May, when asked in some glossy questionnaire 'When is it too old to wear a micromini?', replied: 'Probably sixty, though if you have the legs, go for it.'

Which leaves me considering several options: I can convert to Judaism and claim ancient lineage; move to Japan to join their statistics; train as a New World architect; or buy a micromini. Suddenly I feel that in my seventies life still has lots of possibilities.

~

ORCHESTRAL CONDUCTORS MUST take the same approach. They don't have a problem with age. If they are any good, the world assumes that they will go on being good. The words 'mellow', 'wisdom' and 'experience' feature in reviews of their concerts. Toscanini and Klemperer conducted well into their eighties; Leopold Stokowski gave concerts in his nineties. In my own day Bernard Haitink continues at the helm of the Dresden Staatskapelle in his seventy-sixth year. Charles Mackerras's eightieth birthday celebration concerts continue into 2006. Both remain the toast of critics and audiences love them. No age discrimination there, then.

Nor do we expect conductors to retain their youthful looks: Simon Rattle's tousled locks gave him a boyish charm when he was younger. Now that those tousled locks are grey they bestow a certain eccentric gravitas. Such looks go down well with all who love his work. Pierre Monteux went on conducting the London Symphony Orchestra well into his late eighties, towards the end perched on a stool and making minimal movements. From Monteux we don't expect flamboyant gestures, merely wonderful music, which he regularly delivered.

There was another prominent grey head, recently conspicuously displayed on a number of billboards around the country. It was that of an elderly man, faceless and anonymous, his grey hair thinning, displayed below the message: 'Ignore this poster: it's got grey hair.' And the strapline: 'Ageism exists: help us put a stop to it.' This was a campaign run by Age Concern to tackle what it believes is the last form of legal discrimination and it's begun to have an effect. It has, until now, always been perfectly legal to sack someone for being old. A routine retirement age of sixty had the force of employment legislation. However, new age discrimination regulations, coming into force in October 2006, set a new default retirement age of sixty-five. Compulsory retirement below sixty-five will still be allowed but only if it can be objectively justified and an employer must inform the employee between six and twelve months before the intended date of retirement and give them the opportunity to request to continue working if they so wish. By mid-March 2006 there was a massive response to union calls for strikes among public sector workers who resented the new directive that many of them would still have to work until sixty-five. It isn't everyone's ideal old age, just to go on working in a job that has become routine.

There are many paradoxes in the way our society sees the old. They are somehow regarded, if they're thought of at all, as a minority group who have problems with pensions and varicose veins. The image of them in the media and in advertising is often insulting and contemptuous. I blench every time I see film of aged couples ballroom-dancing in some church hall in what is obviously mid-afternoon. There's nothing wrong with their doing it, it's just that it's such an overused image by newsrooms as a quick shorthand for 'the old'. What about those mountaineers and hill walkers among us? Younger people need reminding that the over-fifties hold 80 per cent of the nation's personal assets. Forty per cent of the population is over fifty and that percentage is growing steadily. Many of us are actively working and there are plenty who resist the mandatory retirement age.

This image of each generation as it is held in the popular imagination is shaped and coloured particularly by the highly persuasive power of marketing and advertising. The difficulty is that these industries are not merely dominated by the young. Their workforce toils in environments where the next new thing – new styles, new idioms – are idolized. The culture of advertising agencies, media enterprises and television companies is of bright, ambitious young people, slickly dressed, groomed to the last eyelash, setting their values by the world of design and appearance, the fashionable, the immediate, the dispensable. And it is they who write and create the advertisements for household goods, for foodstuffs, for leisure pursuits that furnish the visual background to much of our lives, our streets, shops, magazines and programmes. It's not surprising that they so thoroughly misrepresent what the demographics of the country really are. Those with the money and time to enjoy it are the over-fifties.

To redress this damaging mismatch, Age Concern turned to a group of older advertising wizards to create their new campaign. The voluntary team led by Reg Starkey had an average age of fifty-five. Reg himself admitted his industry is ageist: 'Creatives and marketers who are over fifty are treated as has-beens. In advertising, older people are under-represented or portrayed as stereotypes. The cult of youth in advertising is laughable in a society that is growing older.'

What's surprising is that we all know this to be so and the evidence is there to demonstrate that this is the case. Age Concern's own research shows that 49 per cent think the market takes no notice of older consumers. And the outlook is not good. Of those surveyed 75 per cent think that age discrimination against the old will not get better, with 25 per cent actually expecting it to get worse. There are other areas where ageism exists: in matters such as car insurance, job recruitment and breast cancer screening, the old are disadvantaged without any reason. Their needs are as pressing as those of the young, and they are frequently a safer risk. These attitudes simply persist because no one has set out deliberately to change them. Well, they have now.

~

GOOD NEWS! I have two friends who are separately about to become parents. The surprising news is that they are both over fifty: one is fifty-seven and the other sixty-four. The sad news is that while one is surrounded by love and encouragement, the other is being subjected to public abuse and humiliation for daring to want a child. The great difference is, of course, that the fifty-seven-year-old is a woman – the writer, producer and all-round impressive achiever, Lynda La Plante – and the sixty-four-year-old is a man, whose partner, in her forties, is a professional woman with responsibilities outside her home, which she will now be abandoning.

Lynda is the subject of disapproving press comment on every front; my other friend, who lives in Brazil, has a home and a community of happy and supportive relatives and friends eager to help with the baby's care. It's currently the received wisdom that it's fine for men to go siring offspring into their years of senility, while a woman who seeks medical help to conceive after the menopause or, as Lynda has done, seeks to adopt a child whose parents have chosen to give him up, is vilified and scorned as self-indulgent and cruel.

Consider the line-up of wrinkly old men who have become fathers: Pavarotti was sixty-six when his daughter was born; the former Argentinian president Carlos Menem was seventy-three when his beauty queen wife had their child; Clint Eastwood's most recent children came along when he was sixty-three and sixty-six, American author Saul Bellow proved fertile in his eighty-fifth year and incidentally in his fifth marriage. Julio Iglesias Senior became a father at eighty-seven, Des O'Connor is another late dad, as are broadcasters John Humphrys and John Simpson, plus legendary photographer Don McCullin.

Our response? We may find it out of the ordinary – which it is – and even a bit odd – which is also true. But we somehow forbear to pass judgement. We give these men the benefit of the doubt that they will, indeed, love and cherish the child and provide for it as they are able (ageing parents who catch the headlines are often conspicuously rich) and we generally welcome them into the community of doting fathers ready to swap photographs as well as to exaggerate the accomplishments and the beauty of the newcomers to their families.

Not so the older mother. We don't hesitate to judge her and find her wanting. She is selfish in satisfying her need for a child while setting aside concern for its future welfare. If she isn't already an old hag she will be by the time the child is at school, where it will bear the brunt of mockery and ridicule, simply because of her. She will be too tired and clapped out to run sports day races against the other mums, she won't have the patience to stick and glue, to crayon and paint. She will live in a time warp, not knowing the names of current pop groups, or how to handle computers, text messaging and iPods. In fact she is an all-round social menace and it shouldn't be allowed. It just isn't natural.

But what is natural isn't 'natural' any longer. Infertility treatments and donor semen aren't natural either and such medical interventions are now generally accepted as ethical and benign. Men remain fertile throughout their lives, of course, but advances in science now allow women to bear children after the menopause. That buccaneering Italian Dr Antinori treated women in their fifties; in the 1990s I met two of them and accompanied one as she took flowers to lay in gratitude at the shrine of the Virgin Mary. Clearly the local Catholic church had no qualms at the time. Yet when Dr Antinori's other patient, a farmer's wife aged sixty-two, earned her way into *The Guiness Book of Records* as the oldest woman ever to give birth, the Church hierarchy condemned it as a 'horrible and grotesque act'.

Such discrimination between the sexes intensifies with age and is based on stereotypes that, we all acknowledge, are already out of date. Mothers are no longer sweet and tender stay-at-homes who devote every living moment to their children's needs. Their lives must strike a balance between work and family, far better than do those of men whose sense of self is so often determined by their job and their status among their working peers. Women are more flexible in their lifestyles, more capable of multi-tasking, better at networking among other women. They are also more able and willing to ask for and take advice. Above all, they live much longer than men, and will be around for the graduation ceremonies when other youngsters are putting flowers on Daddy's grave. So the odds, as ageing parents, are in the woman's favour. Why then do we smile knowingly at the sexy old fathers, but come over all sanctimonious when older women seek to add a little to their own and other's happiness?

~

IN A DIFFERENT CONTEXT ENTIRELY, that of work, I know when I'm beaten. I know when there's no defence. I know when I'm up against powers beyond my reach, however determined I am. Currently the particular authority is demographics. In 2005 I was unceremoniously dropped by Channel 5 from a new series of theirs called *Rant* because, as they stated baldly (and thanks for that) I am not within 'their audience demographic'. It was a polite – actually not very polite – way of saying I'm out because I'm old. Odd that, because it was they who had approached me and had all but signed me up. But those nice producers I dealt with had been overruled by anonymous people upstairs, the ones with the charts, the statistics, the audience demographics.

The danger, I believe, is one of ghettoization. There is an assumption that young people – say, under thirty-five – want to watch programmes made and presented by young people. There are plenty of them, they swarm across the screens in all their garish colours, foul language and simplistic opinions. But where are the programmes targeted specifically at older people? I challenge you to name just one. I happen to know how the debate among television folk goes because I've been party to some of it. Old people watch all sorts of programmes, tending to the more serious and, in style terms, the more staid. They like documentaries and David Attenborough. It's assumed that programmes made especially for them wouldn't get a larger audience so they don't get commissioned or made. A contemporary of mine, a former distinguished magazine editor, has formatted a promising series called *The It's Never Too Late Show* and is having trouble getting it to a screen near you.

When it comes to age, it isn't the numbers that matter. It's attitude. Research undertaken by the BBC indicated that when people are asked which mindset/age group they identified with, they almost always thought of themselves as belonging in outlook, taste and lifestyle to that group just a little younger than themselves. When I ask the question, and I ask it quite often, 'Why no programmes for older people?' it was crisply explained that no one wants to be identified with such a group, and that older people themselves prefer programmes tailored for a broader audience among whom they are happy to belong. My own breezy claim that seventy is the new fifty bears this out. It is a way of reassuring ourselves that we are not out of date or out of touch.

At the same time controllers and their ilk declare that they take the issue of the old seriously and ask, 'How can we make a series that is about the old, even for the old, but doesn't alienate the rest of the audience?' What they come up with is *Grumpy Old Men* and a programme that I took part in, *Twenty Things I Wish I'd Known before I was Twenty*. Both were lively and popular, but they treated the old as 'them' not 'us', and confirmed a stereotype of old age as being miserable. *Grumpy Old Women* followed. Both *Grumps* are now bestselling books. There's no doubt that the independent company that conceived them – Liberty Bell – has created a winning formula. But is that to be all?

Demographics lead to such stereotypes. I am sure I lurk as a statistic in numerous marketing surveys as someone not likely to wear jeans or high heels, to drive a sports car or drink cocktails, but to prefer cocoa and sherry, to carry a handbag rather than a rucksack, to prefer gardening to rock concerts. Some but not all of these are true. I'm conscious of my own contradictions: I am pleased when such profiles are used by the NHS to offer me flu jabs, but not so thrilled when I'm identified as the consumer of retirement packages and stair lifts. Demographics may itself be judgement-free but it can be taken in evidence and used to make you feel your age.

At Christmas time I am caught by yet another such lasso. The government sends out £200 to old people living alone, to help them with their winter heating bills. Very kind too. Except that payments like this aren't meant for people like me, with the central heating roaring away, insulated lofts and lined curtains at the windows. They're meant to help those living hand to mouth on a wretched pension without money to spare for an extra bar of the electric fire. Last year I tried to return the gift, but the authorities replied that they had 'no mechanism for taking it back'. There must be many like me, and there are certainly plenty who could do with more than the £200. My cheque goes to charity in the hope that it'll reach the needy by some other route. Yet this doesn't obviate the problem, for receiving charity often feels demeaning, whereas when dispensed by government it comes as a right.

Demographics are a blunt instrument. They corral people into their generalizations and treat them as 'the old', 'the disabled', 'the ethnic', 'the rich'. From these spring such concepts as 'middle England', 'disaffected youth', 'the pink pound'. In the process they tend towards the consensual, dragging us kicking and screaming towards the average. I suspect the aged are particularly vulnerable to being so dismissed. 'An ocean of grey heads' I heard one theatre director describe his audience. And he said it with a hint of regret. Yet the old are as diverse, individual and eccentric as any other group. We include Mrs Thatcher, Mick Jagger, Tina Turner, Doris Lessing, Tony Benn and Cleo Laine. No easy generalizations there!

$\sim$

TURNING TO MORE DOMESTIC ISSUES, I have a fridge full of food well past its sell-by date. I shall be cooking and flavouring, feasting and enjoying yoghurts, cheeses, bacon and wilting vegetables long after many a younger person would have binned the lot. Young people do what labels tell them. I am cannier. 'Cui bono?' I ask of my label. To whose benefit is it that I should throw away marginally stale produce and buy shiny bright replacements? Why, the food industry, of course. I regard a sell-by date as its way of avoiding litigation should one of my drooping ingredients give me a tummy bug. 'We told you so, we are not to blame,' the manufacturers will proclaim in court, as I clutch my gut and beg for compensation.

Not so the younger generation. At the stroke of midnight the food languishing in their fridges turns to rotten pumpkins and next morning is unceremoniously thrown out whether edible or not. The spirit of the Blitz still has me in its grip; nothing that can be turned to tasty – or even bland – nourishment should be wasted. There used to be a wonderful stall in Bury St Edmunds market that specialized in food past its sell-by date. It did a roaring trade. Their French cheeses were especially good, the point about French cheese being that the pungent smell is part of its deliciousness, whereas the English are snootily suspicious of anything giving off the faintest whiff.

In 2004, as things were gearing up for that year's general election, the question arose as to whether Michael Howard – at the age of sixty-two – was already past his political sell-by date. Ted Heath, crusty old parliamentarian that he was, suggested that Howard would be too old at sixty-four to be prime minister. My whole instinct was to back the idea of someone in my age range being considered eligible for power. Consider Gladstone, four times prime minister, first at the age of fifty-nine, then subsequently when he was seventy-one, seventy-seven and eighty-six. He made his final speech in the House when he was eighty-five, and still went on to speak out against the Armenian massacres at the age of eighty-seven in the 1890s. Had he shown similar stamina – and got elected – Michael Howard would have had some twenty-three years of parliamentary life ahead of him.

In fact there were reasons that made this all too unlikely. Gladstone was a giant of the Liberal Party with a vision that looked forward towards universal education, a broadening suffrage and even Irish Home Rule. Michael Howard came with a record that suggested attitudes already out of date. In 1988 he was responsible for Clause 28 that banned the 'promoting' of homosexuality. He voted against the lowering of the homosexual age of consent to sixteen. He voted in 1988 in favour of David Alton's private member's bill to limit abortion to eighteen weeks, then went on to oppose giving women statutory maternity rights and refused the EC Directive on maternity leave. Gays and women have moved on since then and don't look upon Michael Howard as someone who helped get them where they are today. Despite his modest attempts at rapprochement with gays, his outlook was basically one that looked backwards towards earlier values. Indeed, he and Gladstone might only have had in common shared views about sex and virtue.

In drawing attention to Michael Howard's age, Edward Heath invited us to examine exactly what that meant. Did his values point forward to the way the world is going, or hark back to less tolerant and less equal times? Would his sell-by date give us a pain that we came to regret, or would he grow into the full maturity of a ripe and satisfying French cheese? In the event, after the agony of another electoral defeat, the Tory Party ditched the oldies and opted for a thirty-eight-year-old much in the Blair mould. But by this time most of us had realized that we already had a Tory prime minister in Blair himself.

Next up for serious ageism was Sir Menzies Campbell, going by the jaunty name of 'Ming' – running at the age of sixty-four for the leadership of the Liberal Democrats, against relative youngsters, Simon Hughes, fifty-four, Chris Huhne, fifty-one, and Mark Oaten, a mere stripling of forty-one.

In my eyes Ming's grace and rigorous mind looked well against his less stylish competitors. The fact that age had little to do with leadership skills was evidenced in the retirement from the job of Charles Kennedy, a mere forty-seven-year-old, but already flawed for the burdens of office. Next to fall was the closest to him in age, Mark Oaten, ambushed by a sex scandal. In the event Ming, the elder, had the staying power and won the day, and those of us in his age range stopped feeling quite so jumpy.

~

I HAVE ALREADY QUESTIONED THE validity of demographics. Now my grouse is with questionnaires. I have just completed one with a good deal of tongue in cheek. Yes, I said, I travelled to the theatre by tube. My age? Twenty-five to thirty-five. Occupation? Florist. All these lies had one good purpose. It's time to begin subverting the system. I grow increasingly suspicious of surveys. There are just too many of them, all packaging and pigeon-holing us into neat marketing categories. Any minute now that particular company will be reporting a rise in theatre-going by London florists in their late twenties, a trend given credibility solely as a result of that survey.

I believe that surveys themselves need examination. They are not value-neutral, laboratory-style findings. They are often compiled in the most infelicitous of circumstances, a passing street encounter, in bad weather between people brandishing clipboards who'd prefer to be doing something else, and the victim passers-by doing their best to avoid eye contact but relenting before the pleadings of the supplicant's 'It will only take a minute.' So why is this far from exact method used as reliable evidence for claims that can frighten us, threaten us, cajole us but rarely reassure us?

Surveys are undertaken for a specific purpose by institutions that consider it money well spent to make an impact. Surveys , if their findings are startling enough, are sure to make headlines and create news. It's a sure way for advertisers and public relations companies to deliver something tangible for their clients, the more startling the better. They already battle to catch the public imagination, promote feature articles and discussion on afternoon television. They seek to fill space – column inches – rich with speculation. What better than a survey: 'Let's get some statistics, issue a report, catch the headlines' – you can hear the cry echoing round the white offices and white desks of trendy promoters. And it works. Over the years they have helped fuel a popular addiction to health and diets that is surely unhealthy in itself. I'm well aware that they can even be used to promote television programmes; I've been party to it myself. Remember the claims: '72 per cent of the population believe in God' and '70 per cent of women give up sex at fifty'?

Not long ago Cancer Research UK told us that only one in five women takes enough exercise to gain health benefits. The same organization posted to me three alarming pieces of paper threatening that 'One in three of us will develop cancer at some point in our lives.' Panic sets in. Am I among the one in three or the one in five? Or possibly both? And if I'm the one in five, will this stop my eventually being the one in three?

Charities are in the business of raising and dispersing funds. The thought arises that it's in their interest to make the facts as threatening as possible. Only then might I divert my funds from helping the blind, or the mentally handicapped into helping, say, any one of the several cancer charities. And which will it be: breast or colon, prostate or lungs? You just can't have it all.

Surveys and questionnaires often tell you what common sense already suggests for a lot less money. A ludicrously obvious report published findings that show fewer children nowadays join in sport at school than once they did. Well, of course they do, because their playing fields have been sold off. What's more, young people prefer sport that is competitive. That can hardly be surprising in a culture drenched in competitive enterprises. Children are caught up in everything from simplistic quizzes and lottery promotions to school league tables. An apparently contradictory finding tells us that the amount of time young people spend taking part in sport has increased from 7.5 hours a week in 1999 to 8.1 hours in 2002. Are these the same children or others? How rigorous are the terms of reference under which such surveys operate? Do they leave loopholes for bored children, faced with having to tick yet more boxes, to subvert the system? Or is it the teachers who tick the boxes? It could make a difference. Of course, none of this reaches the press reports that we read so gullibly. Only the conclusion drawn by some self-important director tells us that 'more must be done' to get young people involved in sport.

Indeed, 'more must be done' is the conclusion we can expect at the end of every survey. 'More' usually means money and possibly, further down the line, yet more surveys. Surveying is a self-perpetuating industry dredging for evidence that will legitimize the claims being made for more funds, money to be raised from us, as taxpayers and individuals, to be spent in our own interests. Frankly, if £2 billion can't make children enjoy sport I suspect nothing can. You'll find them, instead, kicking an old tin around the few remaining recreation grounds, or turning their fleeces into goalposts in some muddy patch of wasteland. Sometimes people just have to invent games for themselves.

Meanwhile four in five women need to get out there gardening, cycling, walking – keen to defy the one in three prediction, doing something that raises the heart rate at least five days a week. How about sex: does that count as exercise? Are you one of the 70 per cent of women who gave up sex at fifty? Don't worry. I simply made that one up.

~

SLOWING DOWN IS HARD TO DO. Now another blow has been struck at the lazy life. A whole swathe of Channel ferries that made the long crossing to western Normandy and Brittany are being cut. And with them go the long lingering pleasures of being at sea with all the prolonged expectation of arriving in a new country. What excitement the five-year-old Mary Queen of Scots must have felt when she stepped ashore at Roscoff – in westernmost Brittany – on her way to marry the Dauphin. And with what different sensations the fleeing Young Pretender landed there after his failed pitch for the English throne in 1746. Arriving in Roscoff – after some eight hours at sea – may soon be an experience lost to us all, at the very moment when more of us with the time are wanting to relish it slowly.

Crossings to Cherbourg, Caen and Le Havre take, by comparison, a mere four or five hours, long enough to savour the pleasure of the journey, even the romance of it all. The noisy loading at the quay, the gradual unwinding that comes with the steady throb of the ship's engines, the gorgeous splash of the sea in the ship's wake, the call of the seagulls, the long view of England's green coastline, the sense above all, that we are an island and an island people still.

Ferries are losing out to the rail link and cheaper flights in the frantic rush to be there, to arrive, to get the journey over and done with. There's little sense that the journey can be part of the enjoyment in its own right. Some twenty minutes were recently cut from the scheduled time on the London to Manchester route by the new tilting trains. I had the chance to try it out. Luxury, indeed. Standard class is so commodious that we felt we had fetched up in first class by mistake. But as for the time saved, what kind of gain is that? Whose life is so significantly improved by being at a meeting, attending a conference, fixing a deal twenty minutes earlier? You might instead have been deep into a good book, or catching the transient beauty of the countryside, a horse frisking in a field, say, or the sun breaking from behind clouds. But no, those in pursuit of career schedules would, even on a train, be deep into laptop calculations or noisy planning on their mobiles.

It's different for those of us on the cusp of work and retirement. We're learning to give up the hustle and bustle of the highways and enjoy the less frantic pleasures of the byways. The clock ceases to be such a tyrant. The step slows to a saunter. It is the time to be, rather than to do. This has some practical consequences for me. In my rushing lifestyle I would always grab the quickest way to get around and one that allowed me to continue working for all but the minutes it took to move from house to taxi, from taxi to destination, especially when the cost could be credited to expenses. This impulse vanishes with age, too. Now, more and more often I get around London by bus and tube. And I can feel it doing me good; my freedom pass allows me totally free travel the length and breadth of the city. I also get the exercise of walking to the station and the bus stop. So by opting for less speed I am benefiting both my pocket and my health. Of course, I'm familiar with the torture of rush-hour crowds and the squalor of many routes, but slowing down means I travel out of peak hours, and some parts of the tube are getting better. There's good busking too.

Slow is already a growing movement. The notion of slow food goes back to a campaign begun in Italy to protect the delights of the table against the depredations of fast food. It's no accident that it all began in Italy. *The Journal of the American Medical Association* recently hailed the Mediterranean diet as beneficial to the elderly. Along with the wise choice of foods goes the habit of eating at a relaxed pace, making the meal an event among colleagues or family, and reducing the need for constant snacking all through the day. I'm signing up for such habits myself.

So how else do I plan to slow down? One way is always to turn up early. There's nothing so exhausting as rushing to be on time, the sweaty panic, the mislaid papers, the careless clothes. If I turn up half an hour early for the train, there's time for a coffee, and don't I need a pair of socks? If I arrive in good time at the theatre or concert hall – the National, say, or the Barbican – there's time to read scholarly programme notes that come too late once you've seen the production or heard the music.

As to the cross-Channel routes, I predict these will make a comeback as luxury outings. They'll get the cruise treatment, decked out with gourmet food, on-board lectures, bookshops and luxury goods; they'll be as much fun as the Orient Express in conjuring up how things used to be. And as we sail away in full view of the white cliffs of Dover, we'll be reminded yet again that we are still an island people.

'No spring, nor summer beauty hath such grace,
As I have seen in one autumnal face.'

JOHN DONNE

TWO

Mirror, Mirror, on the Wall

GROWING OLD MAY be more about the body than the spirit. I'm
confident that many people remain as young in heart as they ever
were and often as sharp in intellect too. The body is the evidence
we see in the mirror. So as we age we are presented with a
dilemma: do we let the body do its worst, knowing that those who
love us will value our inner selves, or do we have regard to how we
look and try to retain something of how we once appeared? The
effort can't go on for ever. You'll notice that beauty lotions and
creams promising to slow the ageing process never feature
models over the age of forty-five. How could they? It would only
demonstrate their ineffectiveness.

Perhaps because I began life as the petted daughter of adoring parents, and as a young woman was well aware that I could use my looks to get favours and opportunities that my wits wouldn't, I still have a care to how I look. The streak of narcissism that goes with a career in television aids and abets this preoccupation. How does the former so-called 'thinking man's crumpet' – my media tag for so many decades – grow old gracefully?

In these pieces I let my vanity show through: embarrassingly so. Here I am making a commercial, here I am being painted. I also talk of what problems we all have with our bodies, how we are judged by our image, how there's a dignity in wrinkles and how the talents of the old can sometimes flower as the years go by.

~

PHYSICAL STAYING POWER gets harder as you get older. It isn't that the body's incapable; it's simply been in use a long time. Each springtime thousands of people will join the London Marathon to run the twenty-six miles through the capital and then collapse in exhausted heaps with the effort of it all. Rather than realize that the whole venture has been a futile waste of time and energy, they will be high with a sense of achievement, cheeks glowing with pride and passion. Both press and television will remark on the oldest people to complete the course and we will all marvel at their stamina. Not many years ago a gentleman in his nineties – with a body that was nothing more than sinew and bone – crossed the finishing line with great dignity and modest bearing. Jaws dropped. He was ninety-two. How did he do it?

The truth is that in age our bodies begin to let us down. No matter how keen we are to keep going, the joints play up, the muscles sag. Those who tend their gardens will find that getting up from their knees takes a little longer than it once did; the tennis players will not have the pace across the court they once had; the walkers will know that unless they keep up the habit their stride will falter. It is a fact of life. It falls particularly hard on those whose careers depend on their being on their feet. Hairdressers and surgeons develop varicose veins; I'm sure teachers take to administration as much to get the chance of a good sit-down as to get the children off their backs. The world moves faster than we do. I steel myself to withstand the rush of people from a crowded Underground tube hurtling themselves towards the exit. I am the last to leave trains, still collecting together my possessions while fellow passengers are already queuing for taxis. What's the hurry? The worldly round of families and careers, rivalries and riches, hopes and ambitions has only one destination, and none of us wants to get there.

That's why the short-term project has such appeal: the book to write, the lectures to attend and, yes, the marathon to train for. Composer Harrison Birtwistle is considering writing another opera. The last one took some ten years and he is now seventy-one. I look forward to the opening night. Lucian Freud certainly has stamina. At the age of eighty-two he produced one of his most intriguing and daring paintings, *The Painter Surprised by a Naked Admirer*. It manages to be both witty and poignant, highly original, yet in the great tradition of the artist and his model. He has pundits from the art world and opinionated media types all vying to interpret and then judge this extraordinary work. Me, I worry about an old man on his feet all day. The painting shows us the artist himself, wiry but slightly stooped, standing back from the canvas, with a naked woman – muse or mistress – coiled round his ankle, clinging, inhibiting his freedom. I'm only glad there's a chair conspicuously in the picture, somewhere he can rest his old bones. Other heavyweight artists have stamina too: Frank Auerbach and Anthony Caro are still in their studios.

I'm constantly impressed by orchestral conductors; I always cite them as inspiring examples. Lifelong musicians like Colin Davis and Pierre Boulez continue to hold places of honour in concert hall programmes and their performances show no decline in attention or insight. Indeed, critics sometimes remark on how the years have mellowed their fastidious styles. Perhaps the physical nature of the work has provided exercise through the years and they simply keep on going. Yet even they will eventually feel time taking its toll. There came the day when Richard Strauss found his stamina running out and he opted to conduct sitting on a stool.

For the rest of us – and, indeed, perhaps for them too – there is now another recourse: the array of potions and tablets, jars and bottles on the shelves of chemists and health shops. We are awash with advice about vitamins and supplements, herbal this and compound that. I start my day with a parade of pills lined up before me: the cod liver oil for my joints, omega 3 and ginkgo biloba in the hope of keeping my memory good; magnesium and vitamin C because someone told me they were beneficial. There's sometimes a dash of echinacea, occasionally acidophilus, and arnica at the ready for when I fall over. I hope I am attentive without being gullible to the whole swathe of compounds and complexes that the pharmacologists are offering us. Given a hefty dose of scepticism about most medicinal claims, I reckon I've nothing to lose. Now I'm being advised to add a daily aspirin. Well, why not, I say!

~

OPEN YOUR MOUTH and I'll tell you how old you are. This has
nothing to do with how you might speak, referring fondly, as you
may, to the wireless and the gramophone. Nor does it relate to not
knowing who the Kaiser Chiefs are. No, this is about dentistry.
What do your teeth say about you?

The old usually have fewer of them, that goes without saying.
But a whole history of dentistry is recorded in a myriad cavities
and bridges, in gums receding like melting ice caps, and evidence,
crying out to the professional eye, of rusty and outdated habits of
dental care. Whenever it was that flossing came in, I never got the
hang of it.

When I was a child a visit to the dentist was genuinely
frightening and painful. Drills hitting raw nerves were all to be
expected. And the extracting of teeth was done with something
akin to a pair of tongs wielded with ferocious glee rather as
they might be in a Hogarthian lampoon. Children would scream
and hide behind their mothers' skirts, only to be dragged to
the inevitable torture. Somehow, although dentistry is well
nigh painfree these days, the shadow of the terror lives on. Say
you have a dentist's appointment and the response is still, 'Poor
you!'

Despite this, my childhood dentist sometimes provided surprising and unintended delights. I remember as a schoolgirl
having a mask clamped over my face and being given a hearty
intake of gas. I remained painfree and happy throughout the
extraction. And I stayed that way, waking to a sense of serene

intoxication that wafted me home floating on air in a delirium of hallucinations. A whiff too many, surely.

By that time, it's probable that both my parents had already lost all their teeth, not to decay entirely but to dental custom, yielding them up in a once-and-for-all operation that was normal in those days. It was seen as nothing more than sensible, practical and economic to undergo one bout of torture rather than drag it out over the years as each tooth gave way. From then on grinning sets of false teeth spent the night in a glass of water by the bed, to be gobbled into place on shrinking gums every morning. Not only did gums shrink, but cheeks caved in, leaving women drawn, even haggard, opening their withered lips to reveal beaming pristine rows of teeth without blemish.

Then came fluoride, lightweight drills and caring dentists. We learnt to love the snaggle teeth we were born with, the Terry-Thomas gaps and minor flaws that give individuality to a winning smile. Naturalism was in. With a little help, that is. My daughter's thumb-sucking left her with prominent teeth and the nickname Bugs Bunny. So the teenage braces had to do their best. Who would ever have predicted that they would one day be a fashion accessory?

Artificiality is back. Serried ranks of crowned teeth grin in unison from the party-goer pages of glossy mags: all the same, all neat, tidy and totally without character, today's version of the gleaming gnashers that sat in the overnight glass on the bedside table. Fellow television journalists in America were appalled that I hadn't had my teeth 'fixed', mumbling not quite out of earshot that British orthodontics (which I still call dentistry) must be in the Dark Ages.

All these reflections are prompted by a recent and final visit to my dentist. Final, not because I have suddenly become the toothless old woman of Camden Town, but because he is giving up the hurly-burly of Camden's National Health Service and making for the sunnier meadows of private practice in Putney. It's a significant parting. It may be fine for policemen and teachers to look little more than teenagers, but when medical people who have had supervision of your body for decades, who have peered into its orifices, heard its gurglings and attended to its problematic rhythms, when they go, then a particularly private physical intimacy is gone. Older people get shy about their bodies. Revealing them to the young is not going to be an easy prospect. I say this through clenched and beautifully maintained teeth.

~

MY EYE WAS CAUGHT BY a cartoon: a pair of high-heeled shiny black boots and set against them was the label: 'Don't even think of it, Grandma.' I knew it was meant for me. In the heart of me there lurks that girlish impulse hankering for the crazy clothes that are totally unsuitable for my age. I have been looking at *Vogue* ever since as sixth formers we gathered in the school library and crowded round the only and rare copy brought into school by someone with a modish mother. Its glossy pages – themselves something to marvel at after the paper scarcities of the war – offered visions of delight and pleasure still also rare in austerity Britain. Things gradually improved and luxury goods became available. In the long run everyone could afford to shop. *Vogue* continued to set the pace – though by then it showed me a world

I recognized. It was a world I also knew to be full of hype and posed glamour, lavish goods deliberately priced high and exotic visions of otherwise ordinary people. Fashion display and photography has gone from strength to strength in recent decades and is now a boom industry. You can probably get a degree in window-dressing. I go on reading the glossies, which have now almost nothing to offer me, except regrets and nostalgia.

I continue to love the sheer effrontery of much modern fashion. I know, too, that you're meant to give up the pantomime for real life and look the part you've found for yourself. I've been engaging with that recently because I have been sitting for my portrait. The first thing I was asked was how I would like to be seen. Instinctively, my unspoken response was corny enough: younger, of course, lithe of limb, slender of form, smooth of skin. Then reality kicked in. In the event, I ditched the scarves and silks, the beads and stuff, and turned out in a faded blue denim shirt. At last I was comfortably myself. Have I arrived at an age when I simply don't care, when I am happy with being me?

The fact is that image matters, and as I watch from a long perspective it seems to matter more and more. It determines a whole range of serious affairs: whom we vote for, whom we believe, whom we admire, whom we emulate. In the 1940s and 1950s the world of information was largely monochrome and male. There were books and newspapers – no colour, few pictures – because the print was always the focus. With the arrival of newsreels and *Picture Post*, the bastion was breached, cheap photographic processing came into its own and for the last half-century we have lived through an orgy of imagery, so dense, so dazzling that we are glutted with its superabundance. Its ironic climax must surely have been a Turner Prize nominee who submitted simply an empty room with a light switching on and off. Hmm, so challenging, we purred, so contemplative.

We have become so finely tuned to the nuances of image. Lectures in how to perform well at a job interview tell young people to be neat and clean, but it goes further than that. Your choice of clothes – of labels, even – can either impress or turn off others. How much more so is this the case in front of the television cameras. In 2005 there was a ripple of newsroom gossip from ITV that Mark Austin, tousled and husky, was being groomed as the heir to Trevor McDonald, stepping ahead of the women in the race, the glamorous Katie Derham and the svelte Andrea Catherwood. Katie and Andrea are lovely women, and they play their glamour to the hilt. They grace grand occasions in fabulous clothes and indulge the pleasure of being admired. But Mark Austin doesn't do that, nor does Trevor McDonald. Nor does any male broadcaster, actor or film star. Although women get the red carpet treatment, it might well impact on their professional chances. Thus can the powers-that-be decide 'women = frivolous', 'men = serious'. And the old divide lives on.

I was caught up in such clichés myself in the 1960s and I would have hoped that by 2006 we'd be less given to judging by appearances. When in the 1970s Angela Rippon kicked up her legs for Morecambe and Wise it was clear that she was never going to present the BBC's election programme. Perhaps the ballroom-dancing Natasha Kaplinsky won't either. The appointment of Emily Maitlis to present BBC Television's *Newsnight* brought with it typical coverage of her looks and fine fashion sense. Sadly it also extended to pictures of her spilling from a glamorous low-cut gown at an award ceremony. This is not a problem for Mark Austin. Treading the fine line between being a fashion icon and a serious current affairs presence is a headache for women to this day.

As we moved towards the 2005 election we were debating images as much as policies. Labour's leading women were seen as 'too posh'. I wondered why three women had been deselected in Tory constituencies when there was such a shortage of candidates. Perhaps the selection committees privately noted the quality of their shoes or registered the streaks in their hair. Did they apply the same tacit assessments to men, I wonder. In 2006 the arrival of David Cameron to lead the Tories made instant news of his youthful looks, his open-necked shirt and the fact that he rides a bicycle. Discussions of his policies only dribbled in later. Meanwhile the slender figure of Condoleezza Rice glides sleekly across Europe and the Middle East, a model of neutral imaging, keeping both her gender and her colour subject to her political presence. In the world of media spin that's a real achievement. Let's hope her diplomacy is as successful.

Where are the old in all this? It's the older electors who tend to vote, so more older candidates might be welcome. There's no upper age limit and the oldest MPs in the House show a blithe disregard for style that is positively endearing. Consider Gwyneth Dunwoody and Peter Tapsell, both confident in their mid-seventies, and, oldest of all, Piara S. Khabra in his eighty-first year. All of them stood again in 2005 and were re-elected. Menzies Campbell, the new and vigorous leader of the Liberal Democrats, is sixty-four. If we want more older MPs, well, *Good Housekeeping* recently declared Honor Blackman the most glamorous woman over seventy. Perhaps she should stand. She'd get my vote. She could even wear those shiny black boots.

~

BBC4, THE ARTS CHANNEL, full of interesting and serious programmes, is one of the BBC's best-kept secrets. That's because it doesn't go in for publicity in the way other celeb-mad channels do; nor does it list the content of programmes in any way that might indicate whether you wanted to watch or not. That's why you probably missed me, which is a pity because I had a message you might well be pleased to hear.

The programme was called *Flowering in Autumn* and it looked at artists in their old age. My interest was sparked by the 2003 Titian exhibition at the National Gallery. Among the fine familiar portraits was a disturbing painting of truly brutal cruelty painted in raw and searing colours: *The Flaying of Marsyas*. This, I learnt, was 'late Titian'. There were others, I learnt, in this 'late style', typified by fluid brushstrokes and an easier, more abstract line. Something changed as Titian grew older. This brought to mind Verdi, whose opera *Falstaff* I regard as one of his greatest, written in a new musical style that abandoned the more formulaic structure of his earlier work for a new and continuing lyricism. Verdi was eighty years old when he wrote it. Again there was some fundamental change in approach.

I went to talk to today's artists, Paula Rego and Harrison Birtwistle among them. Both continue to break new ground in the style they have made their own and that has grown more assured as they have grown older. Both are in their seventies and at the peak of their powers. What is going on? Is there some scientific explanation that accounts for the surge of creativity in older people? And could it apply to the rest of us?

I consulted Professor John Gruzelier of Imperial College who wired me up to take a look at my brainwaves. His theory goes something like this: brainwaves can be deconstructed into different lengths. Those that are longest are called theta waves and these are associated with certain states of mind. Those who practise yoga and meditation produce plenty of theta waves. It has also been found to be linked to creativity. Experiments with orchestral players has shown huge improvements in their musicality once they have focused on their theta waves. These results were not simply a matter of subjective whim but were independently and authoritatively assessed. It begins to look as though creativity itself is allied to theta formations in the brain. I don't think it's anything as obvious as cause and effect but the association is certainly there.

The next link is the important one. It seems that as we grow older – and this applies to all of us, not simply artists – our brains produce more waves in the theta state than used to be the case, and thus make us more receptive to our creative impulses. What might have happened to Titian and Verdi, and may well be happening to Rego and Birtwistle, is that their older brains are more available for the creativity they've spent a lifetime developing. So their current work is a natural progression. There is no sign of their talent dimming, or any impulse to retire. 'What would I do anyway? I don't want to do anything else,' was Paula's reaction. Clearly her theta waves are in the ascendant.

Where does that leave me – and the rest of us? While I was wired up, sounds of water burbling across pebbles were played to me. I was told that whenever my brain moved into the theta state, I would hear the crashing of waves on the seashore. Well, I produced plenty of those waves, and my mind filled with images of great breakers thundering onto the beach. I was lost to the world. So this indicates, it appears, that my theta waves are in good working order. It's now up to me what I do with them.

Over the years it's natural to worry about losing one's memory. At the first sign – forgetting a name, not being able to recall a phone number we've known for years – many of us panic. Perhaps we should put the emphasis elsewhere. Theta waves may well explain why the elderly are thought to be wiser than the young, and why our judgements are seen as carrying a different weight. If we push the idea further, all those evening classes in watercolours, Third Age lectures and Open University courses seem to come at just the right time for us. With children grown up, homes settled and career ambitions laid aside, our lifestyles give us the opportunity to indulge our brains. We have time to allow our minds the space and freedom to explore new territory. How good to know that the science is with us!

~

BRAINS ARE ONE THING, looks quite another. Last year I was in a film directed by Mike Leigh. I know it sounds grand. It's meant to. When I was approached to take part, it was the name of the director that particularly impressed me. Well, it would, wouldn't it? Leigh already had a shelfload of awards for his television plays, and at the time I was approached he was only just back from Hollywood where his film *Vera Drake* had been nominated for an Oscar. Although it hadn't won, its nomination confirmed his standing as one of Britain's finest directors. He wasn't to be refused. Besides, Clint Eastwood was never going to ask.

I should have given it more thought when I so readily agreed. But the cause was good and my trust in the gloss and glamour of cinema is a leftover from the days of Betty Grable. Surely I could expect tactful lighting, the cunningly placed key light designed to flatter, the lens chosen to obscure rather than highlight physical blemishes. All this was blithely in my mind as I went before Mike Leigh's camera. Too late I realized that Mike Leigh doesn't do glamour. I was to discover that his talent for telling the unvarnished truth, as in the stark honesty of *Vera Drake*, was to be deployed on my willing but ageing features.

Breast Cancer Care was launching a major campaign to make women more aware of the support and information that the charity provides for anyone who wants it. From the moment of that dreaded diagnosis, a phone number can put anxious women in touch with all the help and advice they so desperately need. I, along with a number of other women – Cherie Blair, Meera Syal and Denise van Outen among them – agreed to take part in a commercial, directed by Mike Leigh and masterminded by M & C Saatchi, which sets out the Breast Cancer Care promise along with that phone number and website. Of course, this being a good cause, it wasn't seemly, I thought, to allow considerations of vanity to surface. I arrived at the studio to be confronted by a close-up camera, searing in-your-face lights and the gentle persuasiveness of this world-class director. I was simply too timid to challenge the master's authority in the matter of how to look my best, or even reasonably good. My role, as I saw it, was to speak the lines and do as I was told, which I did. The result is not a pretty sight.

That is not the point, of course. There are more serious matters of concern for women of my age. The risk of breast cancer doesn't decline as you grow older, but the opportunity for breast cancer screening does. Somehow I had persuaded myself that once I was past my fifties and sixties the dreaded diagnosis was not going to happen. However, it can and, in fact, is more likely to do so. We need to remain alert. The NHS breast cancer screening programme has just extended the age limit for actually inviting women to be screened to seventy years. Beyond that age you can still be screened, but you have to remember to ask for a referral from your GP. That sounds fine enough because no one is officially deprived. Yet over seventy is a time when our memory goes. On how many occasions do you go upstairs to fetch something and forget what it was? Now, unlike the mere striplings in their fifties who get a reminder in the post, older women are going to have to fend for themselves, putting Post-it notes around the place and entering reminders in diaries.

It's perhaps for this reason that I was invited to be a patron of Breast Cancer Care, to remind my contemporaries that this service is for them too. Perhaps that's why everyone but me is quite happy that I should look my age on the commercial. So there I am alongside the smooth glamour of professional good-lookers like Jerry Hall, the clear-eyed appeal of Lorraine Kelly, the pert attractions of youngsters like Geri Halliwell and Zoe Ball. Do I mind? In a frivolous way I do, because vanity still lingers. And though I look in mirrors these days with fewer expectations, I think it's still important to keep up the impulse that Mike Leigh has so easily undermined.

More seriously, there is a quite natural reason that worries about looking my age are genuinely trivial. Those who have given their time to be in this film have often done it for personal reasons: Cherie Blair's aunt, Jerry Hall's sister, Denise van Outen's grandmother all had breast cancer. So had my sister Susan, who died when she was fifty-nine. Some of the people whom we loved are now gone, denied all chance of growing old. They never even lived to see their wrinkles. And I realize how lucky I am to have mine.

'I grow old ... I grow old ...
I shall wear the bottoms of my trousers rolled.'

T. S. ELIOT

THREE

In the World's Eyes

THE REMARK OF T. S. Eliot's fastidious Prufrock exemplifies the awareness we have that the world is looking at us. We are being judged by how we appear and as we get older it is the young who judge harshly, lumping us all together as not worth their bright censure. In the old mind/body debate we surely know it is the mind that matters. None the less the two interconnect. We can observe that to be so in the way that we can read the character of a friend in their clothes, their manners, their body language, their movements. Indeed, it is those very charms, the loping walk, the toss of the head, the liking for colourful scarves, that encapsulate the personality we know them to have.

In these pieces I battle to hold on to my own identity against the encroaching anonymity of old age, sustaining my wilder tastes while knowing them to be inappropriate, remarking the differences between my own tastes and those of the young, and beginning with a story to chasten anyone who enjoys the freedom to express themselves in their appearance.

~

THE DEATH OF A PRESENTER of British television might merit a routine obituary listing their programmes and distinctions, if any. The report would be noted for the moment, prompt mild regret and then the world moves on. The death of Shaima Rezayee in Afghanistan is entirely different. It deserves to be in the news and remain there, a reminder of the women who struggle to emerge from the stultifying restrictions that they endure in so many countries. The gulf between cultures resides in the lives and often bodies of their women.

Shaima Rezayee was shot in the head on 18 May 2005 at her home in Kabul. Some eight weeks earlier she had been sacked from her job at Tolo Television where she had worked since 2004. Her career was brief but meteoric for in that time she had become the darling of Afghanistan's youth. Shaima was twenty-four years old, pretty and bold; she dared to present a version of the West's MTV, in a country only recently loosened from the grip of the Taliban. She had the courage to show her face publicly alongside her two male colleagues, joking and chatting together as they introduced videos of musical tracks. The music was of all kinds: Iranian, Turkish, Arabic, Western and Afghan. The programme, called *HOP*, exemplified the porous nature of young people's music. Cultural barriers and national boundaries have no meaning in this world. Clearly Shaima loved it; beyond the studio, she wore jeans, drank alcohol, made male friends. She would have been at home on any street in London, Paris, Barcelona or New York. But in her own home town, she was gunned down. She had upset the mullahs and flouted the conservative ways of her country; she had been attacked as anti-Islamic by the Supreme Court and received death threats in the days after her sacking. Two of her brothers were taken into custody. There is the suspicion that it might have been an honour killing. The Director General of UNESCO condemned the murder, declaring: 'On no account can murder be considered an instrument for cultural policy.' Well, no.

How different it all is from the home lives of our own young women. Surely 2005 was the year that launched the revival of the summer skirt. Legs were flashing on every pavement; fake tans were whistling off the shelves, and everyone under thirty-five had long since given up on summer tights. Bare legs – golden and glistening – were the order of the day. Meanwhile belly buttons were still to the fore, builders' cleavages gracing the derrière, while pregnant mums carried all before them like galleons under sail.

Where one culture fears and hides the naked female body, the other celebrates and adorns it, flattering its curves and flesh, decking it with colour and glitter. The streets of the West are often a feast of youthful sensuality and delight. It is not so easy if you're older, or bumpier, or slumpier. As each year passes the fun goes out of fashion for me. I discarded the bikini in my fifties; strappy dresses are no longer within my range; upper arms call for long sleeves. Must I now address the dilemma of bare legs? These, however, are the gripes of a self-regarding, body-conscious culture. Basically we in the West enjoy the freedom to celebrate our skin.

So why are religions so tough on women? In the Victorian heyday of muscular Christianity, the rules of feminine dress would have met the highest standards of the Koran. It was in religiously devout America that Janet Jackson's nipple caused so much fuss. Only as we have become more secular have we shed our clothes and our inhibitions. Who are these gods that they should require their own creatures to be ashamed of their bodies? Granted, there are limits in polite society. An attempt to have topless newsreaders was only ever a porno joke. Nevertheless the notion that the supposed Creator is offended by the natural beauty of his own creation is well nigh blasphemous.

Shaima Rezayee was caught in the clash between a punitive culture that fears and resents women and the new tradition of global music and universal entertainment that celebrates them. If religious extremists of all faiths now want to put the clock back, they will have to reconfigure the role of women as we have, within my lifetime, come to enjoy it. The control of dress might seem a petty matter, but it is loaded with significance. It is for individual women to decide for themselves where along the cultural spectrum – from the easy ways of Western display to the comfort of regular concealment – they choose to live. Whoever says that feminism has had its day?

~

'MUTTON DRESSED AS LAMB' used to be the sneering phrase whispered about ageing women who dressed in younger styles and wore make-up reckoned to help them pass as more youthful than they were. This was considered a sort of generational dishonesty in a world where everyone was obliged to know their place. But no one eats mutton any more, and no one cares a toss for hierarchy and their place in it. What people do care about is being thought old, by which is meant 'out to grass', or 'over the hill'. These phrases apply literally to sheep, but by no means to the present generation of the over-sixties. So what to do?

I was contemplating all this as I sat in the hairdressers decked out with folds of silver paper, putting yet more coloured strands and streaks into my hair. I long ago lost touch with the actual biological colour of my supposed crowning glory. It must be some fifteen or so years ago that it first vanished beneath a tide of henna and auburn, light brown and dark brown. Somewhere at the roots I occasionally glimpse a line of mixed black and white. Pepper and salt it would be called if it ever saw the light of day. Pepper and salt to go with the mutton, that is.

And here they come, the catalogues clattering through the letterbox. Spring fashions dancing like little lambs across the pages: Toast, Boden, Pure, piling up beside the winter's tempting offers of exotic Peruvian knitwear and red thermal vests. I think mail order is great because it means that I shall get to try on the drifts of flimsy summer clothes, the bold T-shirts and plunging bodices displayed in the pages on models younger than my daughter. When you fill in the order form, there is no box requiring 'age'. (Or sex for that matter either; is this how transvestites shop?) I can also avoid the curling lip of derision from young shop assistants biting back the impulse to snatch away garments with 'lamb' written all over them. There is – and there always will be – the chore of sending back the garments that won't suit or don't fit. Trying them on may not have been fun, but at least you got to confront uncomfortable truths in the privacy of your own mirror. So it's back to the Post Office with what I usually reckon will be around 50 per cent of what I've ordered.

More news for spring lambs from the cosmetic counters. Sales of anti-ageing skin treatments have reached a new high. According to a survey by the company Olay – whose own creams rejoice in words such as 'regenerating', 'anti-ageing', and 'nourishing' – women in their thirties and forties spend an average of £200 a year on products to stop their age showing. Two hundred pounds: the same as a pensioner's winter fuel allowance. I wonder whether the spending goes up as women move into their fifties and sixties? Does there come a point when they simply tire of the effort, face the truth and stop taking any trouble at all?

For there is a paradox here, as the old become an ever larger proportion of the population. By 2050, remember, one person in five will be over seventy; that is 12 million of us – and there'll be a further 8 million between sixty and seventy. Being and looking old will be the norm. Springtime will have turned to autumn. If we are to make the case for being old as a plateau of well-being, if more and more Third Agers discover late-flowering talents in adult education, and jet off on Saga holidays to climb Mexican pyramids or ride camels in the desert, then looking old will be much more appealing. The idea of old codgers facing a steady decline into disability and illness will have given way to the concept of old age as a time of benign pursuits and pleasures. There'll be a new generation of sprightly old people, many still working, plenty of them around and about, hell bent on having a good time as well as being useful and vocal in their communities. Looking young might start to seem rather naked and unformed, like those scurrying turtles newly hatched, hurtling clumsily down the beach to find maturity and grace in the swelling oceans. We'll come to give true value to the beauty of such older women as Doris Lessing, Nina Bawden and Baroness Warnock. Perhaps all these vats of gloopy cream will be redundant and mutton will be, well and truly, back on the menu.

Well, I can dream, can't I?

~

MEANWHILE THIS IS HOW IT'S GOING TO BE: 'Eccentric old ladies, wizened vamps and deranged elderly divas' were cited recently in a Sunday colour supplement article as the inspiration for current beauty product colours. It seems that oldie peculiarities are what trendy make-up is now all about. It's always a mistake to open the pages of any magazine about style that has a young bottom featured on the cover. I should know better. The old should keep away from what preoccupies the young. However, a certain defiance tempted me to turn the pages.

Hence I found make-up artist Pat McGrath taking her cue from 'an old woman who'd been locked in a closet for forty years with nothing but a lipstick and eyebrow pencil for cover'. Surely this is ageism with a vengeance, mocking those who can't help being wrinkled in the course of light-hearted waffle about what shallow young things should put on their faces. I was incensed. McGrath wasn't the only culprit. Terry Barber weighed in with more abuse: 'A lot of make-up artists now employ the eccentric touches that mad old ladies have.' This is the equivalent of comparing skeletal fashion models to famine victims.

The fact is that make-up is different as you get older. Glasses become essential to see what you're doing. Eye make-up applied without them can be a pretty hit-or-miss affair. Those hinged make-up glasses don't really do the job. You have to rely on a magnifying glass to the power of five. Even when you score a hit, the contours have shifted since you so smoothly applied the eyeliner twenty years ago and the hand may not be as steady. This deserves sympathy, not mockery. The young are heartless. The lavish application of colour to sagging cheeks risks creating a cross between Miss Havisham and Jean Giraudoux's Madwoman of Chaillot. That's why so many of us simply give up. Older faces most often present a neutral beige to the world, a bland expanse of the safest foundations, lightly topped off with a dredging of paler powder, giving the impression of a frail moth grown too timid to approach the flame.

So where do these make-up babes get their notions? Who are they referring to when they speak of 'unhinged' chic? The only actual diva whose make-up was as memorable off stage as on was Maria Callas, who, having discovered glamour late in life, went overboard with the eyeliner, drawing great sooty lines across her eyelids and into the foothills of her broad Greek brow. Throughout the sadness of a declining career and an unhappy love life she presented the brazen splendour of her face to a merciless world. Are we expecting the young to turn out like her?

I read on, hoping to fuel my fury still further. Instead I began to be charmed by the direction their argument took. Miranda Joyce – another beauty guru – began to soothe my outrage with her more thoughtful views: 'When I look at twenty-year-olds they all look the same. I think as some women get older they become more individualistic and eccentric.' It seems to me that these make-up experts admire a certain defiant individualism. Surely they have Vivienne Westwood in mind? I was consoled further when I remembered the poem Jenny Joseph wrote in the 1950s: 'When I am an old woman I shall wear purple/With a red hat that doesn't go and doesn't suit me.' The point is not merely that her lines celebrate outrageous behaviour in the old – 'I shall spend my pension on brandy and summer gloves/And satin sandals' – but that it was twice voted the nation's favourite post-war poem. It seems I rushed too hastily to judgement, being on the lookout for gratuitous hurts. The feeling among the young seems more to be that old age should be mad and wild, flamboyant and reckless. They are then prepared to indulge our excesses to the extent of copying them, adopting our smudged eyeliners and cottage-loaf hair buns as the latest catwalk innovation.

They are daring us to be bold. Who can resist a challenge? We should rise to the occasion, ditch the acres of beige foundation, the tentative dabs of what our mothers called 'rouge'. We are at an age beyond caring. It's on with the cyclamen pinks, the crazy bright blue eyeshadow. Time to get extravagant with the mousse, the gel, the hairspray. There's no time to be lost if we want to win the flattery of the young and it's there for the taking. Personally I'm considering a silver-topped malacca cane the next time my back gives me trouble.

~

MY MOTHER USED TO DRAPE a dead fox round her shoulders. This was in the 1930s and it was the highest notion of chic. As a child I was fascinated by the creature. It had a strange similarity to picture-book depictions of early man draped in the skins of the wild beasts he had killed, though, of course, I knew my mother hadn't killed the fox herself. We didn't move in such fox-killing circles. People who hunted were, for us, the grand folk who owned things like horses and land, and sent their children away to school. They were as remote from us as Amazonian natives, so there was no question of our envying them, or even giving them a second thought. In those days our world – everyone's world – was very cut off from that of other social groups living within the same country, even the same county.

None the less my mother's wearing of the fur was a gesture of social aspiration. She had probably seen sepia photographs in society magazines of young people like, say, the Mitfords, or the Manners families, in which they were all being gaily abandoned, happy and carefree. Life for my mother was none of these things, but at least she had the symbolic fur. I was even allowed to play with it. The sleek pelt of its body was lined with brown silk: its paws hung loose and helpless. Its mouth could still bite but its grip was that of a Bakelite clip that snapped open and shut around one of the forelegs. It never really occurred to me that it had once been a living creature. It was part of my mother's feminine display.

Times change and I had thought the whole idea of wearing fur was over. I recall the 1970s protests against it and a brilliantly shocking cinema commercial, made by David Bailey, in which gorgeous models parading in furs were suddenly spattered with blood as they swung the garments from their shoulders. At first it was no more than a glimpse that then turned into a cascade on the catwalk. It was horrifying. There was a rally in Trafalgar Square with the wry banner: 'The first person to wear your coat died in it.' We all listened and took notice.

By then, however, I had my own fur jacket, of blond fox fur. I had bought it on a visit to China in the early 1980s, when such things were sold very cheaply and exclusively to tourists. It had a short life. I wore it on just one occasion, setting out to film a television programme, and my producer refused to let me wear it on camera. Why? I asked. 'Because if people see you wearing it, you'll get turds through your letterbox.' Ever since, it has been consigned to the back of the cupboard and it lurks there still. Quite right too.

With the invention of fake fur that looked like the real thing, we came to think that the wearing of the real thing was dying out. I recall being startled at seeing a famous American actress attending the National Theatre in a full-length sable and thinking how old-fashioned she looked. Society progresses, doesn't it? People move from barbaric practices to more civilized values and small incremental improvements in behaviour become the norm. Fake fur demanded no hardship or sacrifice from anyone, so the high moral tone that accompanied wearing it came at no cost.

But what became the received wisdom on furs wasn't forced on anyone. When I travelled in Europe, it was clear to me that wealthy and elegant women in fashionable Paris and Madrid were still wearing their furs and taking pride in their elegance and style. Clearly the British campaign hadn't reached them. Besides, they said, the British have always been odd about animals.

I read that fur is now back in fashion in this country and not all of it is fake. What's more, some of the anti-fur brigade are also anti-fake-fur because it glamorizes the very thing it fakes. Fashion is often transgressive, seeking deliberately to flout the norms of seemly and conventional dressing. At the London Fashion Week in February 2006, the opening show by whizz-kid designer Julien Macdonald had acres of coats and jackets made from chinchilla, sable and mink. Other British designers, like Matthew Williamson and Clements Ribeiro, followed suit. The young models, too young to remember the protests of the 1970s, flaunted the styles with panache and were surprised to be pelted with flour at the post-show party. The younger generation have slipped back easily to the old ways we once deplored.

Whatever happened to progress? Are values simply cyclical, with behaviour that one generation came to see as bad resurfacing generations later among their children who are no longer shocked by it? I would have thought that with the high profile given to animal conservation, with the statistics of dying species so familiar to us, the world would have moved on for good in its treatment of animals. Yet only the other day I received a lavish sales brochure for a luxurious crocodile handbag. Fortunately it cost over £5,000, so I shan't be buying many of those. Again, it gave me pause for thought on the matter of progress. Then I recalled that I need my chimneys sweeping and was wondering whether a small boy might be available.

~

I HAVE ACCIDENTALLY FALLEN FOR A LOGO, which is not something I intended to do. I purchased one of those casual summer bags that are to be found everywhere in shops and magazines but not in my wardrobe. Its loose shaggy shape, made of some kind of denim and hanging from handles that were once associated with knitting, bears a rather striking device: a large serpentine curl, neither letter nor number, that gives it, I thought, a certain style. Imagine my surprise to learn that it is the logo of a particular manufacturer, which turns up regularly all over their merchandise. I should get out more.

This represents something of a defeat for me, for I have long made it a matter of principle never to buy anything bearing the maker's logo. This has little to do with Naomi Klein's fine book *No Logo*, which details the damage that the manufacture of Western branded goods does to the poor countries where they are made. It goes back further than that to days when goods were bought and sold on their intrinsic merits rather than their brand marketing.

When I worked briefly in advertising as a copywriter, I recall it was one among many selling stories to claim 'X wears our clothes', rather in the way that Gary Lineker eats certain crisps. Whoever lent their name to the claim was paid for it. Since then, by some brilliant sleight of hand the advertising world has reversed the process. People now pay money in order to be used as billboards for certain brands of clothing. The more expensive the clothing – scarves, trainers, bags – the more the public seem eager to act as unpaid display space for the company's output. I see no reason why I should do so.

This can make shopping tricky. If you go into any sports shop and ask for tracksuits, sweatshirts or socks without a logo, they will look at you as if you are mad. At best, they will decide you are the props mistress for some wayward amateur theatrical group performing, say, a Jacobean drama where Nike or Adidas would look incongruous or even hint at a directorial irony beyond any audience to decode. Reluctantly they ransack the stock for something plain, retrieving from the neglected shelves at the back one or two lacklustre items that they clearly regard as having no potential buyer. I promptly snap them up.

Was this the problem with Marks and Spencer when its sales took a tumble a year or so back? No conspicuous, persistent logo? No message constantly writ out across our bodies that this is the thing to buy? After all, generations of shoppers have known that they could always count on M & S quality. Their goods have been the bedrock purchases of millions of women for years. Knickers and nighties, T-shirts and trainers, smoked salmon and salads ... all they sell was seen as reliable, trustworthy, reasonably priced. This is now the problem. None of those attributes has any glamour about it. Shopping has become such a high-intensity, self-defining activity that goods that are wholesome and con-sistent simply don't answer the shopping drive. At one time we shopped for things we needed, when we needed them. Now a whole new range of personal satisfactions come into play: self-expression, individuality, inner gratification. It isn't called retail therapy for nothing.

The trouble is that these satisfactions aren't met by the nitty-gritty of well-made and finished articles; they find their fulfilment in the shadowy world of brand imaging, a world that contains many paradoxes and can therefore be manipulated to fool all of us. Take the matter of jeans, for example. Mine are old Levi 901s, purchased years ago on a visit to the States which refuse to wear out. They simply don't count in the world of branding, where jeans of multifarious variations carry fashion's diktat and judgement: jeans low slung or high waisted, frayed or slashed, long or cropped, stonewashed or plain, embroidered or studded with gems. They are all jeans and to an alien would indicate conformity among mortals. Yet the branding sets each design apart. As a function of clothing they are on a par with my own. In branding terms they leave me way behind.

In the logo wars, I want to opt out. Soon the only way to do this will be to revert to the old ways and make things for ourselves. We were once taught dressmaking as a part of domestic science. Girls only of course. We could choose our own patterns from big design books with names like Butterick and McCalls. We chose our own fabrics too, so our individuality was total. No mass markets for us. The skills just about survive: you can see, in the dwindling haberdashery departments of long-established stores, ranks of cotton bobbins and zips, buttons and ribbons, not to mention pinking scissors and boxes of pins. Someone must still be buying them. I feel at home here, reminded of the time when we stuck out for own own style and logos had no call on us. I realize that I've known all along: my new bag is really meant for knitting.

~

STUFF. THERE IS SIMPLY TOO MUCH STUFF. I had just been adding my contribution: more black bags of rubbish on the front doorstep than ever before. As this was almost immediately after Christmas, there was a sort of national climax of stuff. Then the black bags contained other, smaller bags, more colourful, more personal, plus the torn remnants of Christmas wrappings and the shards of all the things that had already been broken. There were tissue and silver foil and the formidable debris from toys packaged so thoroughly no child could find its way inside. There were nonsense and fripperies, jokes, and all the things inside crackers that no one ever keeps. There were the stale leftovers, the half-eaten mince pies and soggy crisps left out overnight. There were the carcasses of various birds, the pork crackling that didn't crackle. It was the appalling waste of an overindulged, benign society that takes delight in giving and simply doesn't know when to stop. Apparently, according to the Environment Agency, at Christmas Britain throws away every year an extra 2.5 million tonnes of rubbish. Meanwhile, in another part of the planet, silent people are sitting on heaps of dust, all that remains of the little they once owned.

No sooner have we got over one frenzy than we're into another, and I have been just as helpless to resist the January sales as I was to resist Christmas. More black bags to the rescue, and the household's collapsing television systems are ditched in favour of something more high-tech. Judging by the confetti of leaflets promoting all things electronic, the industry is frantic to move its rapidly outdated stock to make room for the next wave of innovation. It's already a fashion requirement to have a third-generation mobile phone; how soon before they're on the list of goods considered essential in today's Britain if you're not to be classified as 'living below the poverty line'? And how much faster can the technology get?

I blame the god of choice. Having choice has long been the mantra of conservative economics; it's now the siren call of Labour policies too. Choice itself is seen as an intrinsic good, regardless of what is being chosen. It wasn't always like this. I remember times when we would draw up a shopping list that read 'potatoes, tomatoes, sausages, soap' and get exactly that. Now I see shoppers standing before an array of options, phoning home for help: 'Do you want chorizo, or bratwurst? Shall I get Maris Piper or Desirée?' It all takes energy and effort that could be more usefully deployed in, say, taking a degree at the Open University or running a local Glee Club. And how many like me find that a visit to a coffee shop requires a qualification in risk analysis before asking for the right brew? Whatever happened to 'A cup o'coffee, please, love'?

The utopian view was that 'choice' would unlock all the potential we have for constructing life to our individual tastes. There's not much evidence that it's happening. Instead we seem to have trouble making up our minds, so we follow the lead set by the celebrity culture which more and more favours the tawdry and expensive. I watched, amazed, a television report of the Harrods sale in which a young office worker rejoiced because she'd managed to snatch an unappealing handbag reduced to a mere £250! Presumably she'll make room in her wardrobe by chucking out the almost new, the relatively unworn.

I grew up in a thrift culture. You wore clothes until they wore out; you renewed and repaired, mending laddered stockings, resoling shoes that developed holes. It still irks to see something going to waste. So I'm thankful that where I live we have just the man for the job, a genuine totter who calls round regularly, ringing a great handbell and piling all our old and unloved remnants onto his handcart. Out come the boxes of old stuff, faded clothes, dated fashions. Away they trundle on his contraption, witness to the hoarding instincts of the old, borne off to be recycled in car boot sales, returning to the endless Dantesque circle of hell where people exchange and pass on things no one wants. But even he has grown to realize that there is simply too much stuff. He is becoming selective. The last time he called, he peered inquisitively into the house, asking, 'You don't have any antiques you don't want, do you?' As if.

'No way of thinking or doing, however ancient, can be trusted without proof.'
HENRY DAVID THOREAU

FOUR

Rites of Passage

THE RITUALS OF MY LIFE have long been as routine as everyone's: the changing of the seasons, observing the calendar of Church festivals – all these have followed a familiar trajectory. Daily rituals too are held in common by most of us: we rise, more or less with the sun, spend around eight hours in work, the same in sleep and meander through the rest. Having lived so long, I remember a time when such routines were far more regularly observed. I took part in them virtually without question, as we all did. Churchgoing was part of that, family life too.

Such a pattern has become increasingly disrupted over the years. New social behaviours have made our lives more diverse. Even the landmark big decisions – about our personal domestic circumstances, or significant career moves – are less likely to adhere to some preconceived idea. Marriage, once binding us until death, now comes in serial form. Jobs are no longer for life with a pension at the end. The new cosmopolitan nature of city living, its pavement cafés and late-night entertainments, together with the weekend rush to the country so that more and more people can spend time off among green fields, have broken the unchanging monotony of mid-twentieth-century mores. Yet even with so much change and so much of it enlightened and reasonable, the underlying rhythms still retain their powerful grip. Here are my reflections – often highly sceptical – on some of those patterns and rituals, and their rigorous, if not always benign, hold.

~

IT WOULD BE A DULL SOUL who does not raise a glass on New Year's Eve. Whether it's among a motley crowd of mostly strangers, or sitting alone before the television, surely the ritual deserves acknowledgement. In my memory, the image that lingers is one of clocks: carriage clocks, Victorian railway clocks, the face of Big Ben, strong Roman numerals, neat plain numbers, even the blinking of the digital alarm. Shut your eyes and they emerge from the past, seared on the retina year after year, marking the man-made calendar. 'It's no different from any other day,' say the New Year's equivalents of Scrooge, the wet blankets who go to bed early with cocoa and no companions. But that is to miss the entire point: if we insist a day is different, that in itself is enough to mark it out. In any culture rituals differentiate one day from another. They define our lives.

Indeed, our everyday patterns are driven by them: the feeding rituals of three meals a day, coffee and tea breaks, an evening drink, the final nightcap; the annual rituals of birthdays and anniversaries. Rituals are but the grand forms, habits the daily fodder. Both are the repeating routines by which we count our hours and days. Rites of passage mark the shift from one set of rituals to another. Students give up on the three meals a day; the retired give up the 8.15 to Paddington. Religions have built virtually impregnable rituals to back up implausible stories. That's why so many of us who have given up on the creed still go to church for the carol service and the Easter hymns. There's nothing phoney or bogus about this. The stories themselves carry for the agnostic the message of hope, renewal and salvation, which for Christians is vested in the figure of Christ. Non-believers need that message and its rituals too.

The more multicultural we become, the more other rituals permeate our own. Schoolchildren in Britain now celebrate Diwali, the Jewish and Chinese New Years and probably others I haven't heard of. Western tourists to Madurai throw lumps of butter at giant Hindu gods; the Queen covers her head in a Sikh temple in London. Today it's possible to share colossal ritual events around the world. In the early days of 2005 we were all caught up in the rituals of grief, moving with those personally involved in the Indonesian tsunami along the pathway grief takes, through shock, anger and resignation, finally towards some acceptance of loss. The shared grief found expression in services of remembrance, memorial ceremonies and suchlike. Rituals offer comfort in the bleak world of such random disasters.

Getting older involves a radical shift in rituals. The higher rituals remain, of course, though at Christmas we now sit in the corner nursing a glass of mulled wine, rather than richocheting round the kitchen in a panic of unfamiliar recipes and too many mince pies. Daily rituals that are no more than entrenched habits refuse to budge. How am I to persuade myself that I no longer need the alarm clock to go off at 7 a.m.? When am I to realize that I don't have to work five days in order to enjoy the weekend off? I can work and play just as I like, but try telling that to my inner self. I am only slowly coming to grasp that I don't need an August holiday, but can go when the costs are cheaper, the climate cooler and the beach not swarming with families.

New rituals emerge. Collecting the pension at the post office was once a comforting and regular excursion for many elderly people but it has been snatched from them by the government's wish that everyone should have bank accounts. Plenty of the old don't have and don't want bank accounts. If you've never had one throughout your life, sixty-five is no age to start. The loss of local post offices takes with it a whole host of tiny rituals: applying for licences of all sorts, for currency of different varieties, posting parcels, all that stamping and registering. There was something comforting about those homely queues, with their gossip, observations on the weather, comments, sour and sweet, about the government or neighbours. The loss of village life is to be regretted, but on the other hand health is now transformed for the better by all the rituals of prevention: flu jabs, mammograms, annual check-ups. When were we so looked after even before we become ill?

As each year closes, comes the one ritual that itself endorses change: New Year resolutions. For a shared moment we can turn out the attic of old customs and redundant habits, and try to usher in brand-new ways of doing things. Only the Scrooge who refuses the glass of wine thinks that nothing can change. Even the old don't need to be stuck in their ways. I shall make a start by trying to give up that 7 a.m. alarm call.

~

I CERTAINLY MADE THE PANCAKES. It's an annual routine: the melted butter sliding round the pan, heated to the point just short of turning brown, the batter beaten smooth and pale yellow, then the lift of the liquid in just the right quantity to spread evenly and thin, the nimble flick of the wrist that tosses it into the air and catches the golden disc, ready to dress it with lemon and caster sugar. Who would think the whole process has anything to do with religion?

Shrove Tuesday – pancake day – was the day to eat up the foods that we, as good Christians, would be forgoing for Lent. In such ways do secular traditions cling to once-familiar religious observance. So it still is with Lent. The weeks leading up to Easter are often adopted these days as a prompt for an almost secular diet. I know people who give up alcohol, or puddings, or crisps. No one gives up low-fat yoghurt for Lent. A marker of the Church's year has been taken up by a wholly temporal craze. Piety scarcely comes into it.

I feel the same about royal weddings. They have no further significance for me than a day's television given over to ceremonial: many bells ringing, gilded coaches, the long walk down an aisle of perhaps a glorious cathedral with organ music and choirs at full throttle. Always there are friends and family, women in big hats, men in identikit black outfits, except for the groom who almost certainly will be in military dress with loads of scrambled egg. Later the wave from the balcony, followed by a sigh of relief all round, especially in television's battle stations. It all went well.

In 2005, with the royal wedding of Prince Charles and Camilla Parker Bowles, the pattern was broken. The couple, both having been divorced, had to find a new way to adjust the ritual. The usual flummery of state ceremonies and celebration couldn't take its usual smooth and regular course as it had throughout previous royal nuptials. Princess Anne had taken the vows of her second marriage in a Scottish church, but she was not in line to be head of the Church of England. Charles and Camilla took the town hall route, opting for Windsor Register Office with as much dignity as they could summon. The whole event had an air of being not quite what the country expected. The royal wedding had become a pancake, its once religious connections slipping away.

Times change and that's fine by me. Others had to struggle to deal with what seemed to them a drastic development. For the Church of England whose Supreme Governor Charles will one day be, the royal marriage represented a real crisis. It seems to me they had a legitimate and real problem. Their future Supreme Governor, for reasons we all know and understand, could not take the vows of matrimony before a holy altar in a Christian ritual that regards marriage as one of the great sacraments of the Church. Many clergy believe that either he is with them and of them, or he is not. They asked to discuss this at a session of Synod that same year but were refused. The impression I got was that the

Archbishop of Canterbury, having no doubt taken counsel, came to his decision on his own that a civil ceremony could be followed by a blessing. This was new stuff, breaking entirely new ground. Many in the Synod wanted to at least discuss it. I wondered why they were refused their debate.

The Church is running hard – often in circles – in a bid to keep up with the way the secular world functions. The royal wedding isn't the only example of a fudge that emerges as their way of coping. Consider the issue of women priests. Women have been ordained for ten years now. I reported for television on their struggles throughout the 1990s. These bright and idealistic young women thought the battle was won. Today the passage of time has brought many of them to the career point when they might expect to be made bishops. But still many hardliners object. This is another issue that, as with gays, could threaten a split in the Church. The Synod trod warily, voting merely to discuss the issue again at a later date. Women in the Church of England – as in many religions – have to wait for the men to decide on change.

What's clear is that the established religions simply don't yield to arguments of democracy or justice. If clergy can cite the will of God as determining how society should be organized, then everyone else is stuck with it. God can't be reached to verify his views on every issue that crops up. His ministers on earth – almost universally men – set out whatever interpretation they choose and invoke often hideous retribution on those who don't comply. Women have almost always been on the receiving end, the parameters of their lives, morals, even clothing, determined by religious diktat. Religious change comes over time – centuries rather than decades – and can't keep pace with secular values. If the royal wedding of 2005 did nothing else, it carried change implicit within it. It may even be one of the elements that moves the Church of England towards its ultimate disestablishment from the state. Who knows? God, presumably.

~

I AM A GREAT FAN OF *Wife Swap*. I say this in the teeth of friends and others hissing their dismay: 'What! You can't!' 'Not that rubbish, surely.' Often they haven't seen it and, given the widespread flannel about the concept of dumbing down in the media, have decided this must apply. Perhaps they assume that the programme involves some sexual shenanigans to do with double beds and other people's pyjamas. I will concede on one point: it is a very dumbing-down title. The content, however, is pure social anthropology.

Each week two reckless couples agree to a social experiment whose outcome has me gasping in disbelief at the proof that some people are married to exactly the right person. Given the wayward and hazardous nature of much modern courtship, I am amazed that this has come about. Was it all there in that first thrilling exchange of looks across a crowded room, or have they, buffeted by mortgages and children, simply grown closer and closer? By what psychosexual-social route have they come to be so ideally matched, type for type.

That must be the first question that occurs to the swapping partner who, within days, finds their new spouse difficult, intolerable, even offensive. I'm well aware that the programme makers choose couples with the intention of drawing strong contrasts. None the less I'm surprised at how different the internal patterns and rituals of marriage can be. Tolstoy actually had it wrong. All happy families may resemble one another in being happy, but how they go about it is infinitely varied. What the programme also regularly demonstrates is how less happy marriages develop their own habits and routines, which could do with a good shake-up. As this slowly becomes evident as the programme is being made, some couples benefit at once, coming out of the experience with a determination to make things better. Some actually decide to break up – one, even on camera. It makes spellbinding viewing.

What is true of these exposed marriages is writ large in society in general. There seems to be more and more occasion for people to be offended by someone or something. I admit to being appalled by the degree of swearing in much reality television and indeed in streets, shops and life generally. It seems to have become common to lace your vocabulary with an avalanche of words that were once strictly taboo. In those days there was even a penalty: you were sent out of the class, required to apologize or simply cold-shouldered. Not any more. It's part of the patois of city life and I'm having to get used to it.

Meanwhile an extraordinary range of things seem to cause trouble today. Anne Robinson found you weren't allowed to express dislike of the Welsh. A.A. Gill spoke slightingly of the Germans and was inundated with complaints. That's fine; they are journalists who, as a tribe, trade in the wittier end of abuse. More seriously, people now seem to feel that anything to which they have serious objections should be outlawed. Hence the new swathe of laws to control and inhibit how we speak, eat and spend our leisure. Boris Johnson was sent to Liverpool to apologize for being less than flattering to Scousers. Bizarre.

I grew up in a world where much was not allowed. A glimpse of stocking had only recently stopped being shocking. Low cleavage was still a daring thrill. Nudity on stage and in film, sexual descriptions in novels, theatrical representations of God, Jesus Christ and any member of the royal family were absolutely not allowed. Almost anything on a Sunday was strictly forbidden. Laws and social disapproval saw to that. For decades we battled to have such nonsenses reversed. We saw it as progress that individuals were left to make choices for themselves, to take responsibility for what they wanted to see and do.

I begin to wonder whether we aren't now going back to the old days of control. Could a new tide of puritanism be on the way? Life is going to get very tricky as recent Acts of Parliament outlawing anything that gives offence on religious grounds start to take effect. I think it is a matter of social courtesy not to insult and decry other people's beliefs, but legislation will inevitably produce all sorts of cranky complaints. Are we to be chastised for suggesting that Scientology is a load of bananas, or that the Kaballah cult might have more to do with its modish adherents than inner spirituality? Who, in any case, is to decide? It's the essence of democracy to tolerate not merely those who share your views, but those whose expressed views you find abhorrent. Being offended is part of life. Watch *Wife Swap* and agree with me.

~

I HAVE BEEN DEBATING MONOGAMY. My paean of praise to *Wife Swap* set me thinking about matrimony, especially when I became involved in public debate. I was chairing rather than speaking for or against the motion 'Monogamy is bad for the soul'. This proposition attracted a house-full, people-turned-away crowd to the Royal Geographical Society, among them Hugh Grant and Jemima Khan, who were no doubt in search of reassurance. It is, after all, a matter on which everyone has a point of view, as was made clear by Howard Jacobson when he invited the entire audience of 750 to imagine they were all his harem and how much they would resent being last to receive his favours. It was an occasion both hilarious – with the word 'pussy' being used in a non-feline context in this august building – and serious, when a pretty girl in the audience admitted she had once been part of a harem and it had worked very well.

You stub your toe badly in debate if you can't agree what the words of the motion mean. And so it was with monogamy. Some seemed to think we were debating fidelity to one person at any one time, but allowing for changes over the years. Others took as their definition lifelong marriage to the same person. It seems this latter occurrence is regarded as so rare or so difficult to sustain as to virtually disqualify it from consideration. Yet when it came to it – whichever the interpretation – the final vote went over-whelmingly against the motion. So somewhere within our value system lives the universal wish to be part of one sustained relationship for a lifetime. People want to celebrate their diamond jubilee in a golden glow of children and grandchildren: the apotheosis of a happy life. The ideal lives on.

You have, of course, to be getting on in years to have contemporaries who have already managed to do this. And it's interesting to speculate, given the overwhelming desire to achieve it, what exactly it is that makes marriages last. From purely anecdotal evidence, I tender the following checklist. It helps if each mate comes from an emotionally stable family background. So much is a truism. Equally, coming from a desperately turbulent home can motivate children to make a sustained marriage their life's ambition. I have a friend whose mother had six husbands; in her turn, she deliberately set out to create a loyal home and is still at its heart. Second, it's good to agree from the start on what you expect of life in terms of work, success, lifestyle and family. This is not as easy as once it was, given the modern emphasis on personal growth, shifting employment options, the see-saw of the life/work balance, and the upward and global mobility of jobs.

Next you have to weather the infidelity years. Genetics and biology tell us that men are likely – even programmed – to stray. Social changes mean that women feel increasingly free to do so themselves, or perhaps are less inhibited by society's disapproval. Where at one time infidelity was quietly tolerated, its pain endured, couples are now more likely – and find it easier – to split. Women don't have to put up with philandering partners and, with jobs and incomes of their own, they don't have to. But I have friends who rode out the hormonal years and, looking back, wonder what all the fuss was about. Surviving together the loss of trust is a major rite of passage in a lifelong marriage.

All the long-term couples I know have avoided boredom. This is probably easier today, when women are out and about in the world every bit as much as men, and the 1950s kitchen-sink wife with nothing to say is dying out. An equivalence of intelligence and energy is probably a help. Then there's the matter of parallel or contingent sexualities. It doesn't matter how much, how often or how eccentric, just as long as you both agree; whether partaking in porn, bondage or celibacy, it's the sharing that matters. I have friends with odd arrangements that suit them-selves and perhaps no other. Given our outspokenness about sex, adjustments of this kind must be getting easier.

So on balance, I'd say there's a higher chance for lifelong marriage than we and the sociologists might suppose. The testimonies of those who've got there suggest that, given the will, there's almost no crisis that couples cannot survive together. And the celebrations when they come, bringing together decades of friends to marvel, envy and applaud, are truly wonderful.

~

ANTICIPATION IS ONE of life's great pleasures: a coming event, a promised visit, an expected guest. But anticipation gets thinner as you get older: there are fewer career moves to expect; friends are scattered or infirm; theatrical or musical performances are not, perhaps, as good as once they were, or seem so in memory.

But that makes expectation all the sweeter, and no month does it for me more than July. It's the coming of the formal holiday season – other people's as well as my own – that somehow puts a glow in the air, a sheen of covert excitement. Even now, when people, especially the old, holiday all year round, the prospect of 'the summer holidays' has a unique charge of specialness left over from the almost voluptuous eagerness of childhood.

My mother always began packing a month before departure. The family trunk was fetched from the attic and set out, open, on the floor of the front room (front rooms not being used except for visitors). Each day another offering was placed within its floral lining: a dress newly starched, the wrapped package of a pair of shoes, the rubbery bulk of waterwings. Slowly the lower deck would fill, then the second shelf would be put in place. As the days went by there would be washing and ironing at all hours because we needed to take all the clothes we possessed. Finally, in the week before we travelled, the trunk would be roped, labelled and carted away on a lorry to the local railway station. It would arrive a day ahead of us, deposited into the care of some frumpy boarding house in a side street off the promenade to await our arrival. All this for two weeks in Blackpool, an hour away by train. But I have never known excitement like it.

Nowadays plenty of us travel often and with little fuss, or rather the fuss has transferred elsewhere: the drawn-out tension of a month's packing becomes the hours-long wait at the airport, on the brink of anticipated pleasures but not quite there. Yet the cache of air tickets with their tags and travel advice cannot match the floral-lined trunk of my childhood. Today travel is as much the norm as staying at home. Once it had the quality of something special. People wished you goodbye, good luck, don't forget to write, bring back a souvenir. Today it's hardly worth remarking. Mobile phones and text messaging keep people as locked in personal contact as they are every day. There's none of the rarity of separation that allows a cooler look. Separation is just not being in the same room.

And the old are travelling as never before. I am sent brochures for cruise liners, lecture tours of Greek islands, walking holidays – not too strenuous – in the foothills of the Pyrenees, all clearly targeted at the retired and able-bodied who want to catch up on the places they've missed so far. Sun and sea are for younger spirits. We're on the highways of life, never going to the same place twice, otherwise how will we ever see it all? Those of fainter heart – or frailer strength – have by now found their hotel of choice and go there regularly to be greeted as old friends by the patron and his family.

Yet the getting there gets tougher. Once there were kindly porters at railway stations and trolleys you didn't need to pay for. Now you hump your own suitcase or lose your coins in trolley slots that never pay you back. Whoever invented wheels on luggage is a hero to the old. All the same, you still have to heave it on and off carousels and trundle it miles through Heathrow's convoluted route to the Jubilee line. Now comes a bright new idea from easyJet: the removal of all weight restrictions on hand baggage for all passengers. This is some relief as my on-board luggage is usually excessively loaded with books and shoes. However, there's a caveat: you must be able to lift your bag safely into the overhead locker by yourself, without assistance. They spell it out as brutally as that. It's something I haven't done for years, relying as I do on the kindness of strangers to help me out. The distinction has to be drawn here, of course, between 'Oh dear, please help me, I'm a weak and feeble woman' – an attitude we denounced with the arrival of 1960s feminism – and the genuine plight of an old biddy who hasn't the muscle strength to lift her own luggage. So give us a break, easyJet. You should be training your stewards and encouraging your passengers to help out the old. Then when we disembark at Ibiza or Bilbao, Faro or Naples, we'll be fresh as daisies and as eager as the young to enjoy every minute.

~

EACH YEAR THE Hay-on-Wye book festival leads the field in a summer of similar literary jamborees, and increasingly these gab-fests are places where lively debate and spirited exchanges – not only between writers but among bright and responsive audiences – focus constructively on the issues of the day. In 2005, religion was one such. I had the happy task of engaging in God talk of one kind or another with Stephen Fry and Christopher Hitchens, who were sounding off about the blasphemy laws. Meanwhile Jonathan Freedland explained to me how the Jews manage to be at the same time a race, a culture and a religion; and Jonathan Aitken, while talking about prison life with Erwin James, also touched on the anthologies of prayers he'd been publishing.

At that time government legislation was planned to outlaw incitement to religious hatred, which was expected to cause the most amazing turmoil. This legislation risks being extensively misunderstood. It is there, the government insists, to protect people against attacks and abuse because of their religion. That must, in social terms, surely be a good thing. But there are dangers, in that anyone nursing a grievance that their faith had been insulted could assume they automatically have a case to prosecute. If they are refused – and Tony Blair has indicated that he doesn't expect very many cases to come to trial – such groups will be further affronted, their sense of injury rightly intensified. If prosecutions do go ahead, we can expect to see writers, film-makers, comics, playwrights, novelists and commentators in the dock, defending their right to freedom of expression. With the courts already struggling to cope with their workload, they can well do without a deluge of arty folk choking the corridors of justice, jostling to defend each other and themselves, reducing the whole thing to Ealing comedy mayhem. Would it not be wise, it was asked, to step back and consider, before this charade gets under way?

Back in the 1950s we felt that the world had done with religion. Scientific explanations for biblical miracles, the sense that God hadn't done much about the appalling suffering of recent times, the subsequent collapse in congregation attendances, led many to assume that the old superstitions were gone for good. And for a time it did look as though the secular West was the model for the future. More recently, too, paedophile scandals among priests had resulted in the decimatation of the congregations and the plundering of the coffers of the Catholic Church; failure to adapt to the social mores of the time continues to lock the Church of England in internal wrangles. The Christian Churches aren't likely to be among those seeking prosecutions.

Younger generations don't appreciate just how strictly Christianity once governed our lives. I grew up within the state-established Anglican Church, whose rules took effect in law. All entertainments, shops, even garages closed on Sundays. The figures of Christ and God were not allowed in contemporary plays. In 1942 the Church of England conceded that its insistence on women wearing hats in church might be relaxed as part of the war effort. The most offensive swear words were those that invoked the Deity or his Son. (Lower-case letters were disrespect-ful at all times.) Daily school assemblies were full of prayers and hymns. Non-believers – that meant Jews and Catholics – stayed behind in the classroom. This all-pervading Christian culture was protected by blasphemy laws that are still on the statute book today.

I was wrong about religion. It hasn't gone away. Scientists are suggesting that it is written into our brains. Not surprisingly, in today's multicultural Britain non-Christian religions want equal protection under our blasphemy laws. In my view these laws should simply be repealed. They are in effect a dead letter; the last prose-cution was brought in 1977 by Mary Whitehouse against a gay poem celebrating a centurion's love for Jesus. Twenty-five years later the same poem was read by a multitude of literary people from the steps of St Martin-in-the-Fields, to demonstrate how free we have become. Recently the protest group Christian Voice tried and failed to bring a prosecution against the broadcasting of *Jerry Springer – the Opera*. This is the time to be resolute in defence of the liberal consensus in our own country.

All the more so as, around the world, religions are taking violent action against perceived offence to their beliefs. There have been bombs in two Delhi cinemas in protest against a film that outraged the Sikhs; a Dutch film-maker was shot dead for a transgression against Islam. It is usually the male leaders of the community who lead the attack. All religions inherit a hierarchy of male power that seeks to control and interpret the faith for their followers; it is usually the female voice that is being silenced. The play, *Bechti*, whose production was closed down at Birmingham Repertory Theatre when local Sikh groups threatened to riot, was actually written by one of their own religion, a Sikh woman who was critical of how her own faith operates. If Christianity can still quarrel over women priests, women bishops and celibate clergy, it looks as though religious disputes will be with us for a long time yet.

~

DESPITE MY EFFORTS to break the habit the alarm still goes off daily at 7 a.m. and on comes the radio with the day's news. It's a reflex born from years of being either part of or adjacent to current affairs broadcasting. There's absolutely no need for me to do it any more and dark winter mornings are beastly, but a lifetime of habit dies hard and it has left me with responses that seem quaintly out of date now that the world has moved on.

For example, I still can't believe that Sunday is a day that most people spend shopping. I'm afflicted by an inhibition born of those long gloomy Sundays when nothing remotely associated with pleasure or the spending of money was allowed. Adherence to the law kept shops, cinemas and theatres dark. That's why generations of young people took to their bicycles or hiking boots and headed for the nearest countryside. I recall flocks of cyclists bent double over their handlebars bunched dangerously close like a swarm of insects, their tyres humming appropriately as they sped past in formation to the hilltops of Disley and Buxton. Meanwhile I was in my hiking boots, taking the bus to Hayfield to join gaggles of walkers striding out, and eventually straggling out, along tracks and hillsides. This was the heyday of youth hostelling. Fresh air and exercise were good for you, thus virtuous and permitted.

Then there were the lessons Mother taught, a spin-off from the Sunday taboo: never buy fish on a Monday, because the fishing boats don't sail the previous day so what's in the shops is suspect. This, linked to the sense that there would have been a run on fish on Fridays by devout and observant Catholics, meant we only ate fish midweek. The fact that refrigeration and the collapse of faith have changed all this doesn't affect that moment's hesitation in my mind that something isn't quite right if these habits are defied.

Equally there's reading during the daytime, made especially wicked in the morning when every self-respecting housewife should be dusting and polishing, hoovering, washing, ironing, baking, sewing and mending, until her home is spotless, her body exhausted and her mind vacant. That changed for ever when I had my babies. Once over the turbulence of those opening weeks, I found the babies seemed to do a great deal of sleeping. I took to reading novels. My mother's outrage has lingered with me ever since.

'People just don't read novels in the mornings.'

'But the flat's small, there's nothing else to do.'

'Well, find something useful to do.'

The puritan tradition dies hard. Happily, when judging the Whitbread Prize, I now have the satisfaction, should I need it, of knowing that my morning reading was 'something useful'.

Wickedest of all daytime indulgence is going to the cinema, a conflation of passion and glamour. This dangerous pursuit should really be reserved for evenings and weekends when, under decent constraints, a modicum of naked pleasure is allowed. But cinema-going during the daytime is one of retirement's great pleasures. The seats in these new-fangled multiplexes are usually plush; there are concessions for our age group (waving my cinema and television veteran's card, I can even get in for free!). The popcorn chomping doesn't usually begin until the early evening, so there isn't a miasma of its sickly-sweet smell. And there are some wonderful films to see.

In London we're blessed with the National Film Theatre, which regularly runs films from its archive. I was recently a fan of their James Mason season; before that there were tributes to Patricia Roc and Jean Kent, all legends in my teenage years. Then there was their celebration of Audrey Hepburn ... All of them a gift for those who want to linger in the past. Why weren't the rows packed with white heads?

It's widely assumed that cinema is a young people's entertainment. That's where the huge popularity of cinema-going is supposedly found. It's the audience that the film-makers themselves have in mind. There's plenty that puts off the oldies. They have a sense that all the animation blockbusters and fables are for children, and they may even disapprove of all the thrashing and sucking that goes with the sexually explicit. Yet I defy anyone not to enjoy *Toy Story* and you can always steer clear of Bertolucci. I love the lot. At the peak of my enthusiasm for the cinema, sometime in the late 1950s, I would see three separate films each Saturday: morning, afternoon and evening. So nothing will keep me away now. They'll even offer me a plastic cup of coffee or ice cream or wine to take in. Great!

~

ONCE UPON A TIME there was a story that all British children knew. It told of a wicked man who was part of a Catholic plot to destroy Parliament. He heaped lots of explosives under the Houses of Parliament, was caught just in time, was tortured and then executed, which was just what he deserved. And Britain was saved from its enemies.

Ever since – and we never expected it to change – children have gathered sticks, fallen branches and heaps of autumn leaves, plus the discarded detritus of their modest homes, and built them into garden bonfires. The coincidence of tidying the autumn garden and commemorating the evil deed was not lost on parents who helped the venture along and said exactly where it would be safe to have the blaze. Old sacks, stuffed stockings and crude masks were shaped into a presentable guy that would rival the one next door, or in the next street. Mothers had a specific role, baking ginger parkin bread and making their own brand of treacle toffee, to be taken out and proffered round among friends. (The combination of treacle toffee and woolly gloves led to fluffy food, I remember.) Potatoes were pitched into the heart of the inferno, and retrieved from the glowing embers hours later. A coating of ash on half-baked potatoes was even less appetizing than the fluffy toffee.

To travel by train on the night of 5 November was to enjoy a continuous spectacular, row after row of back gardens, each with its own bonfire and children, scarved and gloved, bounding around the tumbling guy. Sometimes there were accidents.

Warnings were issued, a watchful eye kept, but mostly children had the freedom to take their own risks, to develop, as their temperament decided, a proper sense of caution or responsibility for their own recklessness. It was an invaluable part of growing up, 'play as learning' as I'm sure the teaching textbooks would call it. But then it was spontaneous, taking its place with the other hazardous things we did without supervision, like climbing trees and crossing streams.

Nowadays 5 November has become a formal ritual, taken over not merely by parents but by their representative institutions. After all, who can be bothered with all that earnest collecting of rubbish? Will Dad or even Mum be home from work in time? And whatever became of the recipe for parkin? Now organizations take over. These often civic events are enormously popular. A recent venture planned by Camden Council had to be cancelled because of health and safety concerns about the huge crowds flocking to Primrose Hill. Another year's show costing some £60,000 required special traffic diversion and parking schemes to handle the vast numbers. And once there, the huddled crowds were no more than spectators albeit with cans of beer and the occasional bottle of champagne. I can't help thinking something has been lost.

For a start, the event is rarely celebrated on the night itself – 'Remember, remember, the fifth of November' the rhyme runs, and it's no good if you're doing the remembering on the fourth, say, or the seventh. There has to be a common national convergence for the event to really signify. The whole occasion is now entirely passive, with no effort, no build-up of excitement, no personal participation casting a golden glow of shared achievement. What's more, this is now an occasion shaped by adults and bestowed on children.

Of course there are gains in safety and supervision, but life cannot be lived without risk. The trick is to learn how to deal with it. The latest government notion to criminalize those under eighteen found in possession of fireworks simply makes them ever more dependent on adults and resentful of their rules. Finally, political correctness – not to mention the Northern Ireland peace process – now require us not to vilify Catholics as enemies of the state. But, then, how many children know who Guy Fawkes was any more!

No, 5 November isn't what it was: an opportunity for young people to plan their own entertainment, create their own guys, build rival bonfires, come together with dads to light the blue touchpaper, to marvel at what they have created beyond the nagging patterns laid down by know-all adults. The only trace I can detect of that sense of childhood wonder is the solemn apprehension of a four-year-old boldly holding a lit sparkler at arm's length.

~

OH, HOW THE VOICES HAVE BEEN RAISED, how the choirs have been singing. With Handel's *Elijah* and the golden sounds of the St George's Singers to start off Advent, the pace gathered throughout December 2004 as the carol services got under way. I have always enjoyed singing, and singing songs that are old familiar tunes induces that sense of well-being that sends the spirits soaring. Whether it's 'Danny Boy' or 'Jerusalem', some tingle of physical pleasure throbs through the music. The problem is that I can't sing in tune.

That hasn't stopped me. I first joined a choir at the age of eleven: Norbury Choir, it was called, an adjunct of Norbury parish church of St Thomas's, where I attended Sunday school. The church's resources were meagre, so they put up with people like me, with the caveat that for certain songs I was asked to mime rather than give voice. I failed the audition for my school choir, so the next stop was the choir of Pembroke College Cambridge, where, I suspect, respect for the faith outpaced respect for the notes. And I wasn't asked to mime.

At weddings and funerals I am the one to sing out, in tune or not, proud of knowing the words where others falter, and avoiding the wincing glances of those within earshot. So it is with carols. I can deliver you the third verse of 'In the Bleak Midwinter' at the drop of a hat, while others search the hymn sheet for such an obscure choice. It comes with age, knowing the words of carols.

Carol services are now taking on a different role, as fund-raisers for good causes. Churches across London are booked solid night after night, as different charities mount their own events, marshal their crop of celebrities and pack the pews with people willing to pay to join the singing. What other chance do they get to join massed voices? You can usually find a scattering of sing-along *Messiahs*, one or two *Sounds of Music*, and even an amateur *B Minor Mass*, which sent my daughter home in a state of collapse, as 'it was such hard work'. How much easier to join a carol concert and nudge a little closer to what people refer to as the real point of Christmas.

I have been to two such occasions. Breast Cancer Care regularly sells some 800 seats for St Paul's in Knightsbridge, where you get a candle on entering – one than lasts throughout the service – and a mince pie on leaving. That Christmas, Cilla Black and Michael Parkinson were up there giving readings, and the sight of a congregation lit entirely by candlelight was like something from the eighteenth century, the golden glow mellowing the skin tones and softening the harsh lines of modern dress. The evening raised £36,000.

Next it was the Adfam Carols in St Bride's Church, Fleet Street. Wren's gold and white church takes the breath away and draws the eye in every direction with its beauty. This time it was the turn of Sue MacGregor, Sandi Toksvig and Stephanie Beacham to be among the readers. The charity, which gives support and advice to families with drug and alcohol problems, uses this occasion each year to make awards in its writing competition, where those with close experience of addiction write poems, stories and descriptions of their plight as well as their response to it. This does something to hint that among so much jollity there is real and direct suffering going on. The carol concert serves to connect the two.

Then I attended another service. This time it was in St Martin-in-the-Fields. There was no formal choir and you didn't have to pay. It wasn't crammed with the ripple of pleasure and good cheer. The mood was sombre and thoughtful, focused rather than devout. People weren't there for celebration but to express support for the Guantanamo Human Rights Commission in their efforts to right one of the world's most conspicuous wrongs. Margaret Drabble read poems by Gerard Manley Hopkins, Hari Kunzru read from W. H. Auden, Toby Stephens read pieces by Edwin Muir. There was music too: Philip Quast celebrated our humanity and the Inklein Quartet played music inspired by 9/11. There was no crib, no candles. There were powerful, quietly spoken statements of outrage at the violation of human rights. It happened to be Human Rights Day. And then there was Azmat Begg, father of one of the detainees Moazzam Begg, a father whose son would spend that Christmas in illegal detention, without the prospect of either trial or release. He spoke with modesty, dignity and anger. His account of what his family was going through was the most moving thing I heard that Christmas. It finally put me in mind of what Christianity is supposed to be about. How shameful that those who make so much of their faith should be perpetrating such injustice.

PART TWO

Yesterday

'The great thing about getting older is that you don't lose all
the other ages you've been.'

MADELEINE L'ENGLE

FIVE

Then and Now

OUR SENSE OF TIME CHANGES as we get older. To a small child, the distance between one Christmas and the next seems to stretch for ever. Now Christmas seems to pop up every few minutes. It seems that the dross and debris of one festival are scarcely cleared away before the shops are brandishing the very same tinsel and card designs that we thought we had sent last time round. Time accelerates as it starts to run out on us.

Is the growing speed that we sense an objective, out-there phenomenon, casually called the 'pace of modern living', or is it a subjective, internalized experience that comes with having lived through so many decades? The former is clearly verifiable in the quickening rate at which new technologies come tumbling into the world. My grandparents knew neither the aeroplane, the telephone, nor the radio. They marvelled at motor cars, trams and the mysteries of surgical operations and lived to enjoy the newness of television and washing machines. My parents' lives were transformed by a kitchen full of washers and cleaners, but they had no inkling of the internet, mobile phones or pre-prepared meals. I regard the internet as a miraculous and thrilling new invention. To my grandchildren it's a tool routinely on hand at home and at school.

Did generations in the past experience change in this way? Did grandparents, supping their pints by the log fires of local hostelries, regale the youngsters with what life was like before enclosures fenced off great tracts of common land? Did gnarled old sheep farmers lean on five-bar gates, recalling a time before the mills had sprung up in the valley to take in their wool for weaving and put domestic hand-weavers out of work?

These must have been catastrophic events for the communities concerned, but because they happened over an extended period of time, they were perhaps the single important change within a person's lifetime. In our own era, changes simply keep on coming.

What follows are some reflections on how, within my own threescore years and ten, I have experienced change and how that has coloured my outlook on today's world, an outlook that cannot possibly be shared by younger people who now have greater control of how life around them is organized, governed and moved forward. They, lacking the perspective of the old, make their own choices and mistakes as we once did. Drawing attention to the insights life has given us is not always welcome. So I share them with you here.

~

THE MESSAGE WAS LEFT ON THE ANSWERPHONE: 'Mum, could you let me have your recipe for stuffed marrow?' Stuffed marrow! I hadn't cooked it in twenty years, and the person now making the request clearly cherished some Proustian memory of what it tasted like. I was touched that the recollection of a pretty humdrum dish should have lingered down the years, enough for her to want to offer it up to her own children. I went in search.

Since I am such a hoarder, the recipe must be somewhere. Before cookery books were so numerous and inviting, I used to cut out recipes from glossy magazines. These yellowing cuttings, the lumps of glue now sticking through the all but translucent pages, are stowed away for safe keeping. Indeed, for occasions just such as this. Being asked once in twenty years for such a reference makes it all worth while. The hunt was on.

In the event the cutting came from *Vogue* where Robert Carrier once had a column. Could the recipe be his? I decided to try it out myself. The taste came as a surprise: it was wholesome, nourishing, but almost bland, nothing that would see it survive in today's highly spiced, overflavoured menus. No sprinkling of Parmesan, no freshly ground black pepper, no dash of balsamic vinegar. No dash at all, in fact. It seems the evolution of food has taken us from plain and wholesome to the overcharged taste sensations that colour our takeaways and jazz up commercial ready meals.

At the risk of sounding like Alan Bennett's curate – 'Life is really a great big kitchen; God provides the ingredients and leaves it to us to make the meals' – I began to wonder whether my recipe experience applied to other things. Are we in constant search of the ever more tasty, the pepping up of life? And where will it all end? My evidence, of course, is anecdotal. I am regularly treated to the sympathy of those who think life in the 1950s must have been so dull: no television, no clubs, no wine bars, no visits to Thailand. It wasn't dull at all at the time; we had choirs, and jazz, youth hostelling, tennis clubs, amateur dramatics. There was plenty going on. I'm not sure we would have found binge drinking fun, or clubbing on Ibiza the last word. Such pursuits represent a plaintive search for the ever more outrageous, the further extremes of enjoyment.

Then there's television. Early in my broadcasting life an interview was just that: a long discourse between two people at least one of whom was thought to be worth listening to. No longer: a televised interview in current mode will be intercut with film clips, overlaid pictures, visual asides, all to avoid the charge of blandness, the stuffed marrow of programmes. 'Otherwise it's no more than radio!' goes the cry. But yes it is; the human face expressing ideas, especially a good face and interesting ideas, is fascinating to watch. For evidence see A. J. P. Taylor, Jacob Bronowski, and in our own day David Starkey and Simon Schama. Films too are getting spicier; now we have real rather than simulated sex, passed by the British Board of Film Classification. And I'm aware that pornography is seeking out ever weirder ways of exploiting the human body.

The big question is: does this apply to war? Is there a human need for ever escalating levels of excitement? Would the world without at least the prospect of conflict be a duller place? If we had no invasions or tyrants, no disputed borders or lethal weapons, would we somehow get round to creating them, out of boredom with the stuffed marrow life? Does anyone seriously want to beat swords into ploughshares? Would we give up the risk and glamour of guns for the reliable absence of excitement that is the ploughman's lot? These are all questions that we can refer to the evolutionary psychologists, of course, but it would help to know the answer ourselves.

Meanwhile there are cookery classes in Northampton designed to teach widowers how to cook. In my generation only women ever learnt and practised such skills, so men of my age have been left high and dry by the loss of their wives, unable to boil an egg, iron a teatowel or grill a steak. It's a fine initiative to keep them independent and resourceful. Nothing too spicy, I hope, for their mild appetites. Thankfully the taste for excitement does die away. Perhaps they'd like my recipe for stuffed marrow.

~

I HAVE FOUND MY EXAM PAPERS. In 1950, the last year before A levels began, my generation of sixth formers sat for their Higher School Certificate. I took four subjects: French, Latin, history and geography. And here they are, different colours for different exams, set by the Universities of Manchester, Liverpool, Leeds, Sheffield and Birmingham, presumably for schools in the North of England. We had no idea what the rest of the country was learning. I both loved and hated exams, facing them with fear and exhilaration. The fact that I kept the papers is witness to that. There is, too, something nostalgic about them, a sad, dog-eared testimony to another era. In today's debate they are more than that. Here is actual historical evidence to offer up in the current claim and counter-claim about standards. Have exams got easier?

Well, you be the judge of that. The history paper offered a choice of seventy-five questions in two sections, you had to answer four questions in three hours, at least one from each section. So try these examples: 'Why has Edward I been described as the greatest of the Plantagenets?' 'Did the Pilgrim Fathers achieve their purpose?' 'Do you regard Magna Carta as a great constitutional document?' 'Wherein lay the greatness of Nelson?' And from the geography paper a political time bomb: 'Discuss the contributions of the non-European peoples in the Union of South Africa to the economic life of the country.' It was 1950; the Nationalist Party had been returned to power in South Africa two years earlier and had begun imposing apartheid. I have put a rather tentative tick in pencil next to the question, so I must have thought I knew the answer.

These are wonderfully broad questions; anyone could have a stab at them and go on arguing about them for ever. Answers could in theory range from the childish: 'yes' in response to the one on Magna Carta (why didn't the examiner ask '... and why?') and a 1066 *and All That* answer to the question about Edward I: 'He took Wales, built castles, fought the Scots, loved his wife Eleanor,' all the way to the serious: an essay in *History Today*, an entry in the *Encyclopaedia Britannica* or a scholarly tome published by the Oxford University Press. The fact is that it's not the questions that are hard; it's the answers.

The setting and marking of papers has undergone a revolution since my day. The curriculum has become more prescribed, with teachers having a far more detailed brief of what their pupils can be expected to know. This puts them in a position to teach the answers, rather than to teach the subject. What hasn't changed is a wish on everyone's part for good marks, and I recall a technique that I developed for simply remembering facts – dates and treaties in history, imports and exports in geography – without much considered thought about what they meant. Confronted with such questions as those above, I would be sure to include as many learned facts as possible, no matter how tangential they were to the issue.

Today learning and assessment have been transformed by the inclusion of coursework in results. In my day the honours often went to those who could cram hardest in the final few weeks before exams and organize their thoughts under pressure. A memory jammed with facts served me well, but taught me little about judgement or the true nature of the subject. That would have to wait until university. Now the scope for sixth formers to develop their own ideas favours more worthwhile learning, possibly even for its own sake. Exam results are only part of it.

Even in the big wide world exams aren't everything. A recent survey among leading figures in the media showed that a number of them didn't go to university at all and don't regret it. Instead they went directly to local newspapers, picking up their training along the way, or began as runners and dogsbodies in the world of film and television. What has seen their careers flourish was not a capacity to pass exams, though they may well have had it. Instead they made choices that were more individual, more tailored to their own temperaments, and then, fired up by the will to get going, they had persisted with focused determination. Knowing what you want and going for it seems to me every bit as important as providing learned answers to set questions. Character counts as much as exams in getting where you want to go. And anyway, who said we should all be aiming for the top?

~

MARTIN OFFIAH, the rugby league player, put me right. I'm prepared to admit it. We were appearing on Granada's late-night *The Last Word* and the matter came up of sports TV commentator Ron Atkinson's racist remarks about a black player, made when he believed his microphone was turned off. I maintained that the fact that the phrase ever even rose to his lips showed an instinctive disregard for the values of tolerance that are essential to his role. Martin offered an explanation: 'But he's from a different generation; he can't be held responsible, because that's how they all thought. He's just older.'

Vocabulary changes naturally over time. When we're young we like to think we use the hip phrase, the in slang. That's soon out of date, though, and it doesn't matter. However, in recent decades conscious efforts have been made to change vocabulary deliberately, to put right the insults and attitudes that went with values of the past that we have now discarded. Everyone is required to make an effort in the interests of all. Yet language is one of the first things we learn, and what we learn early and thoroughly is hardest to discard.

So I find myself caught in the same dilemma as Ron Atkinson. I, too, remember a time when there was a colour called 'nigger brown'. I seem to recall it printed on skeins of wool, or bobbins of cotton, possibly tins of paint. To me as a child, it was simply a description of a warm chocolatey brown. There were no black or Asian people where I lived. I'd never even seen any. They cropped up in story books about exotic faraway countries. I knew and loved *Little Black Sambo*, but I made no connection.

I grew to maturity in the decade when the countries of the empire began to win independence. I learnt then that the word 'nigger' was an insult. The correct and dignified word was negro. So be it. I learnt to say 'negro'. Change came rapidly and 'negro' didn't stay around long. 'Coloured' came next, but that didn't prove satisfactory either. Quite how these shifts of vocabulary reached me, I don't know; via the currency of newspapers and television perhaps. I know that it felt right to go along with whatever designation those being described chose for themselves. Who could quarrel with that?

Yet as the politics gained a keener edge, so did people. I recall reporting in the 1990s on a dispute in a London borough that had decided to refer in all its paperwork to 'blacks'. This raised an objection from some in the Sikh community who wanted the term to be the more exact 'Afrocaribbean and Asian'. I don't know where the debate now stands but when I fill in forms from my borough of Camden, under 'ethnic origin' I tick a box marked 'white' and feel its bald inadequacy in describing who I am. With our increasing awareness of origin, I wonder whether I should write 'half-Welsh Stopfordian'.

This difficulty of technology affects other concepts too. Once it was the height of polite observation to call everyone of the female sex a 'lady'; the lower her social standing, the more important it was to do so. With the advent of feminism we were all, from choice, 'women'. But the old jokey habit of referring to a group of females – in offices, say, or at the golf club – as 'the girls' still lingers. And, increasingly, they don't like it. Likewise I would once have been an old age pensioner or OAP for short; now OAPs have graduated to senior citizens and even further, fondly, to 'oldies' – and not so fondly to 'wrinklies'. I'm pleased to see that the *Guardian*'s style book advises that the description 'elderly' should not be used for anyone under seventy.

'Spastic' is now considered a gross insult. It was once merely descriptive of those who over time have been called 'handicapped', 'disabled', or described as having 'learning difficulties' or being 'educationally subnormal'. From personal experience I find this engages the bureaucrats more than the carers who have other things to worry about.

Word diktats threaten to get out of control. I read that one of London's prime opera houses is coming down heavily on the terms 'darling' and 'sweetheart' – words that carry no threat but might conceal the insult of a forgotten name. The rigorous control of language is an arm of totalitarianism and we must remember that. We can all have our preferences but we need to have good reason to impose them on others. My personal hate is 'kids' – it's ugly and demeaning. I always say 'children'. But you don't have to.

~

REUNIONS ARE THE STUFF OF GETTING OLD. As the numbers thin out, those left behind come together in consoling groups to reminisce and to keep at bay the isolation of old age as well as to celebrate past glories. Anniversaries are the superstructure upon which reunions take their shape and no reunion was more heralded on television in 2004 than that of the BBC's own channel, BBC2. I can't believe the date matters much to the public in general, but it furnishes a fine excuse to ransack the archives and take a look at how the entertainers of yesterday have weathered. On BBC2's own celebration, *Happy Birthday BBC2*, it was great to see the young James Bolam of *The Likely Lads*, knowing he was still acting his socks off in the BBC's detective show for 'oldies', *New Tricks*.

BBC2's *Late Night Line-Up* also featured in the two-hour-long marathon. This was nothing, however, compared to our own celebration the following weekend. *Late Night Line-Up* was remarkable in its day – the 1960s – and, though it ended early in the 1970s, the bonds it created between those involved in it remain remarkably strong decades later. For 'everyone' under fifty, *Line-Up* was a live daily programme at the end of BBC2's evening transmission that for almost a decade went out every single night of the year, embracing television, pop groups, poetry, debate, film reviews, and all manner of hybrid talk and anarchy. It couldn't happen today, because its essence was spontaneity and in modern television almost every programme is planned, managed, structured, rehearsed and edited to within an inch of its life and sometimes beyond. Not so *Line-Up*, and it is the very nature of what it was that recently brought together those who had worked on it more than three decades ago.

Some sixty former *Line-Up* colleagues converged on London. People came flying in from New York, California, Australia, Italy, Spain, France and Ireland for the fortieth anniversary of the night the programme first went on air. Considering that it was thirty years since we had all worked together and life has taken us in a myriad different directions, it says something for the friendships we built up all those years ago. It's almost as though we had been in the trenches together.

The best reunions are like that: survivors from the heat of battle. Back in 1994 my old school, Stockport High School for Girls, had a get-together on the centenary of its founding, even though the school itself had been abolished in the rush to comprehensives some twenty years earlier. Such was everyone's sense of loyalty they brought with them old sepia photographs, sports trophies, awards, even the regulation ballooning black gym knickers. The school had been strict, severe even, with exacting teachers and a headmistress who made favourites of those from posher homes. We all had plenty to say to each other about our shared experiences since and how they had shaped our lives. Ageing faces were suddenly familiar – mannerisms, voices, even girlish giggles unchanged by the years.

Reunions face us with our younger selves, not only in the features of the survivors and the welcome false flattery of 'Oh, you haven't changed a bit,' but also in the realization that we were different in the past. And so were the times. There's grim satisfaction to be had in sneering at the troubles and tribulations of the present: the clogged roads, the sullen teenagers, fast food in public places, reality television, the irritant of mobile phones, the impact of global warming. But then we had skies heavy with pollution: cigarette smoking, too, was common wherever you went. Steam trains simply added to the fug. There were draughts and chilblains, measles and whooping cough. There were Russian missiles trained on our cities and no safety belts in cars.

Do things improve with time? The plain fact is some do, some don't. The equation can always be written, subjectively, in favour of the one or the other. Yet those of us who have witnessed the passing years can't avoid the sense that the same mistakes keep recurring: in our private lives this means family quarrels, broken marriages, disaffected children, disappointing careers. And in public life too, with deluded politicians, power-hungry news-papers, money flexing its muscles, invasions, trade-offs and the recurring talk of peace. But for some of us our mistakes, like our years, are largely behind us, which makes coming together to survey how we have survived so very consoling.

~

I HAVE NEVER much believed in slowing down. It doesn't come easily. Our metabolisms all work at different rates and mine seems to favour the frantic, even hyperactive end of the spectrum. It has led to a frenetic, sometimes dynamic style of life that leaves in its wake a trail of projects half begun, letters written and not posted, facts asserted but not verified, ideas launched but not followed through. But out of the maelstrom I have snatched enough variety to provide an interesting life to look back on and the momentum to keep me going when others advise that, at my age, I can expect to slow down. I see no reason to start yet.

Take yesterday for example. I was at the gym by 8 a.m. I have for twelve years now been an enthusiast for the exercise discipline known as Pilates. I was keen on it long before its current modish celebrity, at a time when people asked whether it rhymed with 'pirates'. I still go twice a week and with increasing dedication. I have much to thank it for. It keeps muscles toned, halts that ageing stoop and helps out when joints begin to creak and the back to groan.

By 10.30 I was at Broadcasting House where, despite having swung through its doors for some forty years now, I am still, as a freelance, required to line up at the desk for a visitor's pass. Producers who are decades younger vouch for the fact that I am not a potential terrorist. With the Radio 3 recording over – for a series called *Belief* – I am off to one of the most celebratory events in the old person's calendar, the Oldie Awards ceremony, held over a lavish lunch at Simpson's in the Strand.

Unlike the Oscars this is an event without the tensions and anxieties that go with the competitiveness of youth. Old scores – if they ever existed – have been settled long ago. The glamour stakes are low, no one vests their identity in a display of plunging satin and the treacherous hazards of six-inch heels. There is a benign sense of friendship even for people we hardly know. Here is Eric Sykes, a master comedian still delivering admirable performances of Chekhov; here is Peter O'Toole, the fine features still holding their golden beauty, but relaxed now and given to laughter. John Mortimer is in his wheelchair, George Melly takes the stairs slowly, but neither lets this inhibit their love of gossip and good company. Those veterans of the great days of broadcasting – Charles Wheeler and Sandy Gall – come along. Martin Bell is of the company as is Maureen Lipman and June Whitfield. All are there to celebrate the achievements of the old.

Perhaps the most eccentric Oldie award, as Mountaineer of the Year, goes to Lindis Percy, the sixty-one-year-old grandmother who scaled the heights of Buckingham Palace gates to protest at President Bush's visit to the Queen. Other winners are more orthodox but just as deserving: Critic of the Year goes to the

Guardian's own television guru, Nancy Banks-Smith; Politician of the Year is Tam Dalyell; Explorer of the Year is Professor Colin Pillinger (he of the lost space probe *Beagle*); and Campaigner of the Year is Nina Bawden, who is in relentless pursuit of those responsible for the Potters Bar rail crash that killed her husband. Finally, the top award goes to Sir Ranulph Fiennes (sixty that week) who, even after a recent heart attack, ran seven marathons in seven continents in as many days. None of them gets any media mention remotely comparable to those often vacuous Oscars, which is why I commend them to you now. As the population gets older, the Oldie Awards must surely be destined to register more boldly on our national radar.

By contrast I spent my evening among the young and hip. This was not an aberration on my part, but shows how much, despite the wilful attempts of pollsters and analysts to categorize us by age, the generations can enjoy the same pleasures and each other's company. I was at the launch at Tate Britain of the show called In-A-Gadda-Da-Vida. I hoped you wouldn't ask but the title refers to a track from Iron Butterfly made in 1968 ostensibly called 'In the Garden of Eden' but which, because the rock band was so stoned, transmuted into the more psychedelic version. The show was pretty psychedelic itself, with work by Damien Hirst, Sarah Lucas and Angus Fairhurst offering within a single space a rich commentary on humanity, death, decay, corruption and myth. Not much joy there though. Joy, it seems, is left to the Oldies.

~

EARLY IN THE NEW YEAR I paid off a debt, a really big debt, one that had been hanging over me for some time. And it felt good, like a cleansing of my conscience. The burden of it was lifted and I could walk with a lighter step.

We are all conditioned by our upbringing and one of the precepts of my childhood was that debt was an unqualified bad thing. Such was the disapproval surrounding it, we were told, that adults who borrowed money were punished by having to pay a penalty. It was called interest, and went to whomever had done the lending. The borrowing and subsequent return of toys and books was a measure of good behaviour. We were given little stickers of ownership – ex-libris (though we didn't know what it meant) – to remind forgetful borrowers that the owner was constantly vigilant of their obligation. Libraries gave us lots of practice; borrowing was allowed by the authorities but only if we had a special card and agreed to be fined for overstepping the date. It was a punishment that weighed heavily on light purses.

Shakespeare reinforced the view, 'Neither a borrower nor a lender be,' the advice of that nagging father Polonius, whose other precepts seemed sound enough – all about friendship and hoops of steel – so why not this one? At school, Shylock came as a shock. He lends money to Bassanio against the surety of Antonio's trading fleet and, when it is shipwrecked, insists on his bond, in flesh rather than ducats. The matter is referred to arbitration, which by means of the sophistry of Portia manages to undermine Shylock's identity and life. The point was taken: borrowing – and lending – gets people into trouble.

All this is apropos tuition fees. The future of our universities seems to hang on the willingness of young people to take on huge burdens of debt at just that time in life when they need to be fancy free. In my experience it's in those years following university that young people need time and space to survey the world, drift around a little perhaps, try out this kind of work, get a taste of that career. Will they settle for an active, physical life, or a staid steady routine? Do their preferences lie in being among colleagues, in noisy and stimulating settings, or are they happier brooding alone over statistics and strategies? Do they want to mend pipes or broken hearts? Would they enjoy standing in front of a classroom, or standing all day snipping people's hair? These are the delicious days of being young and making choices. The way your personality finally sorts out which way to go will determine your quality of life for decades to come. The wrong choice and you will grow into a fretful and complaining adult. Matters of debt simply shouldn't come into it.

Many young people today are mindful of money all the time, and society conspires to make them even more so. What effect will this have? In my day the imperative would have been to make the paying off of debt a priority. I come from that puritanical strand of lower-middle-class aspiration that didn't like to be beholden to anyone. So the debt would have weighed heavy, as a moral obligation. We can't heap such burdens on young people. Yet the more I read, the more I can appreciate that some form of tuition fees are going to be necessary.

My old-fashioned view of debt is going to have to change. Debt must now be seen as, if not exactly a good thing, then something

to be taken on without too much angst, to be put low on the prior-
ities, not getting in the way of skiing holidays, glamorous clothes
and such. That's how it is already in the economy, of course.
Consumer spending props up the economy whether individuals
can afford it or not. But for the burden of debt not to be intolerable, people will have to take their obligations lightly.

They will find ways of delaying repayment, negotiating income
that falls just short of payback levels, dodging and weaving
through the system to minimize the damage inflicted on their
lifestyles. Can this really be an appropriate attitude for citizens to
have? Oh dear, I think I'll stop now; I sense the phrase 'moral
fibre' coming on.

~

WHAT GOES AROUND COMES AROUND. It was intriguing to watch
Nanny Frost in Channel 4's self-help programme reviving all the
old techniques we once used to bring up our children, plus, of
course, some neat ideas of her own. Into completely chaotic
families she moves with quiet resolve, imposing simple, regular
patterns of behaviour that give children – who until then have
been running rings round their bewildered parents – a sudden
sense of someone in control. Of course, Nanny Frost is depicted
as some starched gorgon from another age. The production
company have her in a severe dark uniform; they set her up
marching sternly to her task, and play foreboding music as she
arrives. But take away the production fanfares and Nanny Frost,
with her swinging hair and London accent, has a manner not

unlike the firm but friendly style recommended by that guru of 1960s child-rearing, Benjamin Spock. He expressed identical sentiments and attitudes, but in an entirely different context. The wheel has come full circle.

Suddenly I realize that's true of much television. Whenever I discuss my own experience of television in public places I am always asked what I think about dumbing down. So over recent weeks I've kept the phrase in mind while I've been watching the box. Of course, there are glaring examples of inanities beyond belief, *Big Brother* being the prototype. But what people usually mean – what I mean – by dumbing down are programmes whose ideas are not stimulating or challenging in the way programmes once seemed to be. Didn't we once have a much greater number of current affairs programmes? Yes, we did. Weren't there once far more serious single television plays? Yes, there were. Wasn't there a time when arts programmes were regularly given a more conspicuous place in the schedules? Yes, there was. But if we examine the social context of those programmes, they reflected the tastes of an audience keen to broaden its horizons further by taking an informed interest in the world and its culture. Television was then judged to be doing what the BBC's founders intended it to do: to inform, educate and entertain. Television was a medium of self-improvement.

What goes around comes around. Television is still helping people change their lives. I have watched a raft of programmes that are often summarily dismissed by the critics as dumbing down – only to discover, at the heart of many of them, advice and counsel, tips and recommendations about making life better. The level of this advice can be called in question. I hate with a hearty loathing the make-overs that turn decent semis into gothic boudoirs, and homely kitchens into nautical theme parks. But in *How Clean is your House* Aggie and Kim, who cut a swathe through the dirtiest houses in the land, also pass on their old-style wisdom. My own household has upped its use of vinegar as a result. Likewise the dreaded Trinny and Susannah, telling us *What Not to Wear*, seem to me to have cock-eyed tastes, but they manhandle women into a direct and fearless encounter with their own bodies that will surely help them feel better about themselves. Self-improvement is on every hand; there are programmes that urge you to clear out the backlog of junk in the spare room or alert you to the risks of moving abroad, chasing a false dream; programmes that teach you about property values; programmes that demonstrate how marriages survive and adapt. They are all classes in life skills.

For people who would rather watch a *Horizon* special about stem cell research, or a critique of Bach sonatas by Murray Perahia, these programmes are indeed dumbed down. They do not play to AB audiences with highbrow tastes, who either employ others to sort out life's housekeeping for them, or who enjoy a casual, slightly rackety way of life rather than invite someone else's attempt to groom them. (I count myself among this latter group, incidentally.)

This is the problem. The end result of so many similar programmes about how you and I might live and dress and cook and decorate is that we could all end up looking like mail order models living inside an Ikea catalogue. Have you noticed how the straight men given a make-over by the five gay guys always become somehow just one of the crowd, losing their shaggy locks, their weird dens, their dishevelled clothes, and in the interest of what exactly? No, I reject the term dumbing down; it's inaccurate. But can we please have our serious programmes back? Then, sitting fashionably dressed in our spotless, tidy and freshly decorated homes, everyone can enjoy a decent single play or a programme about stem cell research.

'This aged England ... she has a secret vigour and a pulse like a cannon.'

RALPH WALDO EMERSON

SIX

Englishness

I'VE NEVER HAD ANY DOUBT about what it means to be English, or rather what my being English means to me. It is inevitably born of my background and my first growing awareness of things. Basically my early life was defined very locally; I grew up shaped by my family, my school and my church. That's how things were in the 1930s and 1940s. This background was at once socially and emotionally stable, and intellectually coherent, and therefore, almost as a consequence of those two, intellectually unchallenging. Taken together, family, school and Church shared the same values and attitude to the world around them. They all pointed in the same direction and were confident enough not only to believe that it was the correct one, but to exert gentle but persistent pressure on me to accept that world too. There was little challenge but much reassurance. These ideas were expressed almost geographically in the part of England I knew.

What I took for granted, but have increasingly seen as intrinsically English, was a modest, discreet and seemly society, little given to expressing emotion, but doggedly confident that the values they lived by had been hard won and would not be shaken. This stubbornness hardened during the war, alleviated by a grim humour about the enemy and utter conviction of final victory. Somewhere beyond the seas, but bound by authentic ties of empire, I knew that there were lots of other places whose peoples paid allegiance to the same monarch and Church as I did. That sense of security, due to the sheer scale and numbers and the certainty they provided, was profound. Even when I became aware of its ruthless history and continuing contradictions, I still held fast to that Englishness from which I sprang, ashamed of its faults, proud of its virtues, but – and this is the point – never in doubt as to what it was.

There was another strand of my identity too. Living near Manchester and the industrial North when it was still in full and powerful sway, I was conscious of its fine radical tradition. The Chartists had been this way; the Pankhursts were local heroines; and Mrs Gaskell's novels had uncovered the wretchedness of Victorian life, which cried out for social remedies. My grandfather had heard Gladstone speak on his final election campaign at the age of eighty-five. My grandparents toiled in the shadow of belching chimneys and roaring foundries, but they had a native pride, even a cussedness, that defined the race. At the same time, living also on the borders of Derbyshire, to paraphrase the psalmist, 'I lifted up mine eyes unto the hills: from whence cometh my help.' I believed in that strength. I regarded the great backbone of the Pennine range as the country's spine. I loved the rolling, treeless moors, the bleak indomitable landscapes. Wordsworth came as no surprise to me; he merely put into words that sense of exhilaration I always felt as I walked and rambled, climbed ... and got lost in the mist. Later in the softer South I knew kinder places and loved, in the work of John Sell Cotman, John Constable and Samuel Palmer, the gentle light and changing skies that are typically English. These thoughts inform what follows – a variety of ideas, each prompted at some fleeting moment by what I felt to be my Englishness.

~

THE EVENING BEFORE the summer solstice in 2005, I walked on one of England's most ancient places. The sandy heath was cooling from the day's heat. Pine cones littered the ground beneath tall trees. Skylarks climbed overhead. Beyond, the flat curving estuary of the River Deben. Spread before me were the nineteen burial mounds of England's Saxon kings. Here, in 1939, evidence was uncovered of an ancient burial ship with rich and gorgeous treasure, proof that a mighty dynasty had come to rest at Sutton Hoo.

It's now common discourse to debate exactly what it means to be English. Once it was clear enough: if you grew up during the war, with Churchill's cadences ringing in your ears, you had no doubt. It was 'us' against 'them'; a child's talk taking on an awful reality. After the war, things became more complex as the empire

claimed and sometimes fought for its independence, and its subjects came windrushing over here with stars in their eyes about the
welcome they would get. Since then there has been a progressive
loss of confidence in who we are. The term 'mongrel race' is used
disparagingly as though we should want to be thoroughbreds.
Eurosceptics would have us defend our legal sovereignty against
encroaching powers beyond our shores. The Anglo-Saxon kings
might well have experienced the same pressures.

I have come to Sutton Hoo to talk about *Beowulf*, the most
important surviving work of Anglo-Saxon poetry. It is written in
what is virtually a foreign language (which here is just about
holding its own in the craze for cutting university courses,
although American academe is mad about it) and it can tell us
something about being English today. Beowulf is an heroic
warrior who engages single-handed in three great struggles:
against the monster Grendel; against his hag of a mother; and, in
his old age, against the fire-breathing dragon. He dies a glorious
death having defeated them all. But this grand story is set within
a political context of warring tribes: southern Sweden, Denmark
and Frisia (now part of northern Holland) were all either at war
with each other or combining in alliances to defeat the other. So
what's new? The message down the centuries is that the Anglo-
Saxons were already making dynastic marriages to either
amalgamate or resist, just as we today negotiate our way into or
out of Europe. For Grendel read Common Agricultural Policy. It
was ever thus. Being English is to stick up for the mix of peoples
who inhabit our corner of Europe.

So what else do I sense as I survey the land where other
Beowulfs may have lain? What makes this such an English scene?
I don't exclude Scotland and Wales from these thoughts and were

I standing in Glencoe or on the Gower peninsula, I should apply them there too. For what characterizes them all is our sense that a great deal has happened here a very long time ago and has left its mark. The landscape, a product of weather and man, yields at almost every turn a hill fort, an ancient dyke, a stretch of Roman straight road, a tumulus or a barrow where undiscovered riches may still lie. Aerial photographs across the Midlands reveal the pattern of medieval strip farming. Ours being such a small-scale countryside, nowhere is the density of historical evidence so great. Take a metal detector to your garden and you risk coming up with a hoard of old coins (it's a risk, because if they're ancient, they aren't automatically yours). Stand still on a summer evening and hear the beat of Kipling's ghostly rider where once there was a road through the woods.

Archaeology tells us who we are better than any diplomat or negotiator. The evidence is implacable. People living in disputed territories know this to be true. Palestinians have long complained of Israel's systematic destruction of Palestinian archaeology. Australian aborigines have to fight to retain the traces on the land that have marked it out for centuries as their own. To uncover the artefacts and homes of your ancestors is to establish a claim.

The Sutton Hoo treasure itself now lies in the British Museum. Here, in the intricacy of armour and jewellery, the artefacts of trade, in themselves evidence of a structured society, warrior-led and successful, we can come to know who was on this land long before us. And back in Suffolk, as traffic on the A12 hums in the distance, there is quieter and more meaningful testimony to our national identity lying just across the fields.

~

THE PLEASURES OF high summer are everywhere at hand. The freshness of spring green has not quite yet disappeared beneath the city dust. The philadelphus scents the air, the borders are awash with colour. Above all it is the roses, blooming in every hedge and garden, gathered in jugs and set on tables, that epitomize uniquely what the English love about their gardens.

Do we enjoy gardens more as we get older? I recall the playwright Dennis Potter, interviewed in his final weeks, speaking of how the cherry blossom had seemed even frothier, more glorious for knowing he would not see it in flower again. But when the poets mention roses – which they do often – it is usually to remark on the transience of their blooms. From Herrick's 'Gather ye rosebuds while ye may' and Dowson's 'They are not long, the days of wine and roses' to Eliot's 'moment in the rose garden', the rose, in bud and then full blown, captures the fleeting quality of our lives. Yet it is not always a happy tale. Any woman past her prime might echo Cleopatra's cry: 'Against the blown rose may they stop their nose,/ That kneel'd unto the buds.'

How paradoxical, then, that older people cherish gardens and flowers, the swiftness of whose passing can only emphasize the decay of all things. Even more, anyone who has seen an abandoned garden revert to the wild, its paths overgrown, brambles choking hollyhocks and ground elder creeping across flower beds, will know at once how vain it is to try to tame nature. Footprints in the sands of time, it isn't. The chances are that what most garden-ers leave behind is a transitory arrangement of flower and leaf that nature will take over and even wipe out. All that effort gone.

Yet the old seem to relish not only gardens but gardening. The latter I have never understood. Gardening – the real work of digging and hoeing, transplanting and watering – always seems to me like housework out of doors. I have done with the scrubbing of floors long since, so the laying of turf or the digging over of a flower bed holds no charms whatsoever. Yet the elderly are at it like beavers, their kneeling mats, trugs, gardening gloves and aprons, their compost heaps and hedge trimmers, replicating all the paraphernalia of indoor hard labour. They are transported into a world of pleasure and fulfilment simply by stepping across the threshold from the shadowy indoors into the open air and a world of soil and plants. What amazes me even more is that at a time when knee joints are stiffening and backs beginning to twinge, they persist for hours in putting their limbs through the rigours of weeding and pruning, the hefting of wheelbarrows and watering cans. (Mind you, I meet up with them at the gym later, dealing with their subsequent aches and pains.) I can guess that, with few exceptions, a safe gift for anyone over sixty will be a book about lawns or flower beds or, of course, roses. What's more, much of it will be in Latin.

Gardens created by others are an entirely different pleasure. From Regent's Park to Stourhead, the big ones are best. It is even better if they bear the imprint of some creative spirit, able through wealth or fame to bequeath their gardens into the care of others. I was recently at Charleston, the home of Vanessa Bell and the meeting place for many of the Bloomsbury group and its descendants. The gardens there are a joy, the cool of the lake, the sunny paved corner, the dappled shade . . . every variety of leafy experience. It brought a poem, again, to mind: Marvell's 'green thought in a green

come your way when you stay with friends. The entire reception staff and all the dining-room staff with one exception spoke English with a broken accent. 'Broken' gives the impression of something gone wrong. And, indeed, there may be those who think that the Queen's English, which nowadays seems only to be spoken by the Queen herself, or so-called 'Received Pronunciation', which isn't received anywhere you'd want to go, are both being grossly abused by the lilting, twisting dance that the English language now does on a myriad different tongues. I find it delightful. In fact, the hotel's only local English speaker was a dour lad who merely mumbled and brought people the wrong breakfasts.

There was a time when the BBC agonized about the sound of the human voice. I once auditioned at Bush House for the job of broadcasting on the different language wavebands transmitted in the middle of the night to Eastern Europe. (Not exactly a full-time job.) This being the Cold War, the task had a hint of the subversive about it. I failed to qualify because traces of my original speech patterns with the open vowels of a northern accent marred my delivery. Just a few years earlier the BBC had dared the bold experiment of having Wilfred Pickles, a northern comic and entertainer, read the news in a thoroughly Yorkshire accent. The ensuing row split the nation. Clearly they weren't going to take any chances with me in Bulgaria or Hungary, where dissidents eager for news of the West might be put off by a flat A.

Now the times have brought the wheel full circle and today my voice is considered irredeemably 'posh'. (How proud my mother would be that those elocution lessons had at last paid off.) That's fine for Radio 3 and 4, possibly BBC4, but no one sounding like me appears on any channel whose remit is pop music, popular culture or light entertainment, without being mightily mocked.

Those footballers' wives all come from Essex or South London.

So when will these newcomers from Europe and beyond, with their prettily diverse accents, start to make it in the media? Or are we reserving only the more poorly paid service jobs for them? Certainly that's where I come into contact with them and have a chance to learn something of their lives. It's almost always a pleasure. A waitress in the Courtauld Galleries' café comes from the Balkans. Not only did she serve fractious children with a smile, she also discussed the paintings on the walls – a children's competition, not a selection of Impressionists – and joined us in discussing their merits. Recently I was stopped in the street by someone asking in a broken Russian accent the whereabouts of a local café. I was proffered a scruffy piece of paper bearing a sketchy address that had the air of having travelled a long way. At the revelation that he had all but arrived, my questioner broke into a broad and grateful smile and went on his way positively bouncing with delight.

Encounters like these are the reality of immigration. So many of the people coming here are youthful and full of youth's optimism. They are pleased to have arrived, eager to work and to be accepted. Their presence is transforming the mood of wine bars and shops, of cafés and hotels. The surliness and indifference that we have grown used to in Britain is being pushed aside. This new influx is lifting the service industries out of the trough of resentment and ill-humour that infects so many who were born here. The sounds they produce may not always be mellifluous to our ears. I have a personal resistance to the upward inflection at a sentence's end that I somehow identify with Australian nurses, but if it goes with a breezy greeting and a smile I won't quibble. The varieties of Englishness now in the air, offering clues to their origins, hinting at interesting backgrounds, must now be as broad as at any time in our history. How Shakespeare and Chaucer would have loved to hear it: their language, vividly spoken, alive and ever changing.

~

SOMEHOW I ALWAYS end up watching it: *The Eurovision Song Contest*. I see it coming and resolve to avoid it. I know it's the essence of naff, the music platitudinous and the presentation garish. But something about its kitschiness draws me to it. Once it has begun, I feel the smug pleasure of recognition confirming why I hate it. Except that I don't hate it any more. I see it as some frozen moment of how we were and what we aspired to. It has a naivety left over from a more innocent age. It's a part of television's own archaeology, the strata of different eras laid down, yielding to the knowing viewer its clues to shifting allegiances and loyalties.

In May 2004 I sat down to watch the same jaded format, but what sprang to life was the new Europe: thirty-six countries voting and their choices revealing new affiliations. As usual there was the familiar political tit-for-tat: Germany voted for Turkey and Turkey for Germany; Cyprus voted for Greece, Greece for Cyprus. But what a line-up the Eastern countries made against the puny presence of old Europe; France, Britain and Ireland got hardly a look-in. What came striding through with the vigour of a new world were the former Balkan and former Soviet states, all voting for each other. Who would have expected Serbia and

Montenegro to be so popular? What solidarity, too, between Poland voting for the Ukraine, and the Ukraine for Russia. At one moment the Russian presenter used a telling phrase, commending 'our Slavic neighbours'.

All this has little to do with music. I was backing the Streisand-like sound of Cyprus's entry, which did quite well. But what carried the day was the all-dancing, leather-and-thongs show put on by the Ukraine. You felt the wind gusting in from the steppes, Genghis Khan leading the rout. My wobbly geography might have got this all wrong, but that just shows my blurry grasp of what Eastern Europe is about. If it did nothing else, the Eurovision Song Contest tipped me off about a new individuality and thrust from the East that makes Western Europe look insipid, like pale English floral prints in the Mediterranean blaze.

I first knew Europe as a wretched and pitiable place. Hitler's occupation had cowed once-proud countries, leaving only brave little Britain holding out against the mighty Hun. When that colours your childhood it seems natural to believe that everything must focus around your own country, an attitude that plays to the self-regarding nature of being young. Unhappily such thinking has hung around for far too long in much of our political mindset.

Then came the Europe of seasickness and passports, as we made our first post-war, cross-Channel visits. So locked were we into our immediate past that the priority on a scholarship visit to Holland was the laying of a wreath at the Arnhem memorial. But Europe, we discovered, was a network of frontiers and controls. Guards woke us in the middle of the night as the train crossed from France to Switzerland. Later we woke to checked tablecloths and crisp rolls at a Swiss station.

Our pity for our damaged neighbours was more than

compensated for by the discovery that they had strange ways and a glorious culture. How odd, we thought, to eat meals out in the open; the sight of pavement tables got our Brownie box cameras clicking. They ate exotic food like spaghetti and garlic; they dined at odd times, breaking with what I'd imagined was the universal convention of high tea at six o'clock. As we travelled south I made a pleasing discovery: these were beautiful people, golden and lithe, comfortable with a natural sensuality that was missing from our chill Northern selves. The focus shifted and I came to realize that we weren't at the centre of all that was best. Far from it.

Now we are all Europeans. Hairdressers own homes in France, garage proprietors retire to villas in Spain. Leaflets for flats in the Algarve shower through my letterbox. The euro crosses frontiers, leaving us stumbling to convert back to sterling where we once juggled marks and francs. And yet who of my generation regularly looks to the East? It has taken a tacky song contest to wake me up to the realities. They tell me the best place to buy at the moment is Slovenia.

~

THE BRITISH, APPARENTLY, are shy about asking for money. As any fund-raiser knows, the knack is in 'the ask'. If you have the knack you get the money. The rest of us are turned ignominiously away or consoled with the offer of a limp cheque far below the hoped-for largesse. I know of one genius of a fund-raiser who asks in the millions and has been known to return to 'the ask' at once when the sum donated was a million less than he'd anticipated. He was not disappointed. Not many us have the nerve.

That's why the English love the sponsored event. Where you wouldn't knock on doors cold and rattle a collecting box at neighbours or friends, if you offer to put yourself through some strenuous ordeal your well-wishers are only too happy to shell out at the prospect of your suffering. There is usually a curious would-be contractual arrangement where you sign up for, say, £5 a mile on a piece of paper – scanning the list of previous sub-scribers to detect the going rate – and then send off the collector to do their swim or cycle or marathon. Being of a suspicious mind, I always wonder how many of these charitable feats are actually carried through.

My own attitude is: don't bother. I usually hand over the money up-front and then explain that I don't want them calling round with authentication from teachers or scout masters that they have actually performed their designated task. I mean, how much effort does it need to collect £20? I struggle to understand the mind of the challengers. Are they thinking, I'd like to walk from Land's End to home anyway, so why not do it for charity, gain some approval, and boost my self-esteem? Or is their pet project so dear to them that they will stretch creaking limbs, swap comfy desk and armchair for wind and rain, putting themselves through misery in order to do good? This latter smacks of old-fashioned puritanism, which is in short supply these days and therefore to be welcomed.

However, I worry about their health. Older people, having more time on their hands than the rest and perhaps eager to sustain a profile in their community, are peculiarly available to be sponsored. The London Marathon displays numbers of them, no doubt with medical approval, struggling towards the finishing line with gaunt limbs and sunken cheeks. Worthy, indeed, but is it wise?

Two friends of mine were recently so engaged. Stanley Johnson, a doughty sixty-four-year-old, completed a three-day walk of some sixty miles between Exmoor and Dartmoor. Bell-ringers in the churches of Winsford and Widecombe needed help with repairs to bell-ropes and bell-wheels. What could be a more delightful or deserving enterprise? The fact that Stanley – father of Boris – was at the time the selected prospective Conservative candidate for Teignbridge and was keen to promote his presence in the area added only a frisson of political self-interest. For me bells and friendship come before politics.

Angela Glendenning was into far greater extremes of effort. Hitting her seventieth birthday in December 2004, she planned to celebrate – if that's the word – by setting herself feats of physical achievement that would daunt the most reckless. Her plan went in sevens: seventy miles walking; seventy miles cycling; seven miles canoeing; seven miles horse riding. And that's not the end: climbing seven tors on Dartmoor, speaking in seven churches ... so it went on. And all this on one kidney. Angela had recently donated a kidney to her niece Sarah and was doing these things to raise not only money but the profile of the Organ Donor Register.

All this throws open the more serious general issue: of whether old people have organs they don't need any more. (No sniggering at the back, please.) I know of a number of kidney donations made by parents for their children. I've even been present at such an operation and been assured by the surgeons and medical staff that the human body can function fully on one kidney. With the increase in road safety and hence fewer accidents, fewer organs are available. Could this be an alternative source? It is not likely, I suppose. I, for one, feel that while I would steel myself to go through the procedure for the benefit of one of my family, I am too squeamish and too selfish to make the gesture for a total stranger. Besides, I did once look into the matter of donating organs after my death. I discovered that age is no inhibitor from joining the NHS Organ Donor Register. What determines which bits of me get used is the condition they are in. If my organs are too raddled by drink and high living, or simply in poor shape through wear and tear, then other tissue may be used. Skin can come in useful. So can corneas.

~

I HAVE BEEN INDULGING THAT most civilized of pleasures: spending time with books. More specifically, I have been enjoying the reassuring comfort and civic confidence of libraries. There is no environment, apart perhaps from the English parish church, where I feel more grounded, closer to the values that govern my life. But of course, much is changing in both places. That said, the Church of England is striving to shore up collapsing congregation numbers, seeking to reinvent its appeal while at the same time repelling many homosexuals and thwarting dedicated women priests who want to progress to being bishops. In the long term they are, I would predict, on a hiding to nothing.

With libraries, the situation is different. The much headlined news of their decline may have been premature. There are a multitude of conflicting statistics that show either libraries are now little more than video technology centres with a few books attached or that book-borrowing is back and the corner has been turned. Perhaps the changing nature of library life explains the discrepancies. Certainly there is a spirit of optimism at the new Jubilee Library in Brighton where I have been whiling away the hours.

This is a gloriously confident building that was rightly in the running in 2005 for the prestigious Stirling Prize, awarded each year by the Royal Institute of British Architects. Architecturally it has both position and style. It faces a new square, at the heart of what Brighton likes to call its cultural quarter, its bold glass front declaring a commitment to the city well borne out by the wealth within. Here, hitherto unsung, is a collection of 45,000 valuable historic volumes, including an early nineteenth-century treatise on shampooing. Soon, thanks to a Heritage lottery grant, this impressive collection will be digitally catalogued, adding it to the world feast of books available to all.

The earliest library opened to the public in Britain is said to have been the Jacobean library of Manchester's Chetham's School of Music. Marx is believed to have studied there when he was collaborating with the Manchester businessman Friedrich Engels on economic theories that would change the world. Early in the last century, when Chetham's was still a school for poor boys, my father and his brothers, recently orphaned, won places there and would, in later life, speak with awe of the hallowed respect in which the library was held by pupils and teachers alike. Perhaps I inherited that sense of awe. I feel the impulse to fall silent as I enter a library as much as I do on entering a church.

The rule of silence reinforced that sense of respect. Only in a Catholic church with the host on the altar was such profound silence expected. As a schoolgirl I would rendezvous with boyfriends between the stacks at Stockport Library, knowing that the merest whisper would have me thrown out. Oh, the thrill of such trysts! But, even in a state of suburban sexual excitement, I still knew there was something special about that silence, a reverential regard for the learning of centuries that surrounded us.

Before long I was to relish and fear the mighty abundance of the great Cambridge University Library. Its scale and range were intimidating; its welcome had to be earned. From there I graduated to the great rotunda within the British Museum. Marx had been there too, as had plenty of others. It's hard to imagine a time when books were both the primary and the ultimate source of knowledge and were cherished as such. When I visited China in the early 1980s the Chinese made clear their respect for our library system; in India a decade later I saw that the libraries started up under the Raj were still held in high regard. The New York Public Library is one of the joys of visiting Manhattan. The new British Library, opened in St Pancras in 1998, justifies all the fuss there was at the time about its cost, its design and the building delays. Today its Humanities Reading Room breathes with a silence of such intensity that it's almost sacrilege to ask for a book.

Then electronics changed everything. Just as in the 1960s cinemas had been outmoded by television, so it was thought the reading of books would collapse before the advance of information technology. Many of us felt uneasy and sceptical at the prospect of reading a book from the computer screen, but the youngsters said that's how it would be. Local libraries everywhere came under threat of closure. We had to fight for ours and won. But just as cinema survived television, so have books survived the internet. Art-houses and multiplexes fought to bring cinema back

'God gave us memory so that we might have roses in December.'

J. M. BARRIE

SEVEN

Looking Back

NOSTALGIA IS A WONDERFULLY uninhibited sensation. It sits by log fires, relishing the cream tea and scones; it chuckles at antimacassars and sugar tongs, grows wistful at the sight of an Austin 7 or an E-type Jaguar, and sings along with the Ovaltinies, or *Monday Night at Eight O'clock*. It is not good company for the young, for it grows prolix in its anecdotes, repetitive in its recollections and has an irritating habit of offering words of supposed wisdom for which remembrances of *The Goon Show* and the Coronation do not qualify it. But let's go there all the same.

The fact is that like a worn old slipper nostalgia slips on easily, settling into the mind with the comfort of familiarity. It is a regular homecoming, opening the door, yet again, on memories and sensations that we like to keep burnished. Nostalgia casts a golden glow over who we are and where we have come from. If I am nostalgic for the smoky skies of 1940s Stockport it is not that I regret their passing or would wish any part of them back. It is that straining at the nuances of memory, I catch hold for a moment of a lumpy and awkward schoolgirl, scuffing the wet pavements with untidy shoes but dreaming such dreams as carried her far beyond the smoke. Today it is the recollection of the smoke and the wet pavement that bring to mind the joy and freedom of those dreams.

Nostalgia isn't intellectually rigorous; it distorts and amplifies. The past, of course, has more to offer us than simple indulgence. In looking back, nostalgia gazes with pleasure and a sense of melancholy, rather than searching out stern lessons to be learnt. Here, I hope, are some of those pleasures with only the gentlest tinge of regret.

~

ODD, ISN'T IT, how familiar things can slip away when you aren't looking? Let your attention wander and suddenly they aren't there any more. What you took for granted as a pillar of your way of life vanishes, unlamented. Whatever happened to afternoon tea? It used to come along at about half past four in the afternoon, a spread of small crust-trimmed sandwiches and iced cakes, served on flowered china and glass cake-stands. In 1950s Cambridge the Dorothy Café held tea dances where you quick-stepped with gawky youths somewhere between the sandwiches and the cakes. The last time I looked, only the Ritz Hotel served such meals, but that was some time ago and they were always fully booked. Although seaside hotels try to keep the tradition going, which is a nice surprise, somehow today's experience can't recapture sensations that linger in the memory. Gone, too, is all the paraphernalia: milk jugs, tea cosies, doilies ... the latter a gesture of lower-class aspiration to gentility. Now people take a break with a mug, a teabag and milk from the carton. Things aren't what they were.

Coal fires: they've gone and good riddance, all that pollution and coal dust. But I can't forget how wonderfully warming they were, glowing red, mottling our shins when we sat too close and burning the teacakes. (Whatever happened to toasting forks by the way?) No wonder one of the patriotic songs of the First World War was 'Keep the Home Fires Burning'. Now we have radiators, naked and clean, and rooms without a focus, nothing to sit round except the television.

Manners have gone, too, we all know that, although how can men raise their hats to ladies if they aren't wearing one? And what was such supposed gallantry all about anyway? For my father, a stickler for such etiquette, it meant walking the streets with his arm going up, down, up, down, his trilby constantly in the air rather than warming his head. Male behaviour was a mass of petty observances: the opening of doors – of cars as well as rooms, walking on the outside of the pavement, giving up seats in public places, paying for meals, fetching drinks. Then along came equality and we women had to do it all for ourselves. At least we could keep our hats on, though by then they were out of fashion.

Talking to strangers: now we don't do that any more. In the North of England, where I spent my childhood, it was simply what you did. Mothers warned children not to accept sweets or invitations, yet on buses and trains, in queues and waiting rooms, people of all ages passed what was called the time of day. By the hippie 1960s informality flourished and it became routine to talk to anyone, man! The mood of benign trust, an almost con-spiratorial sense that we were all bringing about the revolution, made casual friends of everyone. You might well go for a drink with someone you had met on the Tube. Where does that attitude survive today other than at pop concerts and festivals? Not in my world, certainly.

A general awareness of the Church's year, Sunday observance, banks that closed at 3 p. m., whistling in the street – they've all faded. None of it matters much, slipping out of our way of life to pop up only in nostalgic pieces such as this. But there are changes going on that matter in a far more profound way. We're currently living through such a time, when small incremental changes are being made to our laws that amount to far more than a shift in taste or technology. As a student I delved into the response of Pitt's government to the French Revolution. The outbreak of the Terror across the Channel in 1794 alarmed the English who welcomed the émigré aristocrats but kept out Republicans with an Aliens Act that was the first of all kinds of punitive legislation. It became an act of treason to speak or write inflammatory speeches, to hold political meetings, to bring the king and his government into contempt. Above all, the right of habeas corpus – no imprisonment without trial – was suspended.

Does all this sound familiar? Our government is covering the same ground again. The suspension of habeas corpus is an ominous move that rankles in the hearts of many democrats. As it did in 1794, so it does today. People protested then and they're doing so now. This is a right that must not go the way of coal fires, or teacakes, slipping away unnoticed. We need to hang on to it. The good news is that with Britain's victory over Napoleon in 1815, the political situation calmed down and the right of habeas corpus was reinstated, although most of the repressive legislation stayed in force until 1824. The bad news is that our current war on terror is more abstract than straightforward revolution. How will we know when it's over and who will tell us? It will be a sad day if we ever accept changes such as these as inevitable and merely look back nostalgically to the time when we enjoyed habeas corpus as a right.

~

I THINK IT'S THE APRONS that do it, those crisp white pinafores with frilly straps that cross over at the back before tying in a bow there. They have a Laura Ashley-meets-*The Railway Children* air to them. They are usually thought of as being worn by both children and maids early in the last century. Until a Monday in 2005, that is, when at the funeral of the Duke of Devonshire the estate servants lined the route in deference and many of the women, wholesome and buxom in their trim black uniforms, were wearing those same white aprons.

The habit of wearing black for a funeral was once universal. Hat and gloves were also de rigueur. And it was the custom in our street for each house to draw the curtains in the front room when the hearse arrived at the house of the bereaved. They remained closed throughout the day while the family were at church and afterwards when they returned home for the traditional ham tea.

Only then might the women of the grieving household take down their aprons from the hooks on the back of the kitchen door to protect their funeral clothes from splashes and spills. You never knew how soon you might need your best black again; one or two of the aged aunts could be looking frail.

There were rules about aprons. The wraparound overalls, that covered everything and tied with two strings, fitted through a hole under the arm, were considered appropriate only for hard work, scrubbing floors and such. They were usually made of cheap cretonne in small floral patterns and were regarded as lower in the social scale than what I can now call the Devonshire apron, although even these were strictly for indoors, to be hastily discarded whenever someone came to the front door. My mother would peer through the curtains to see whether the caller merited the no-apron greeting, in which case she would snatch it swiftly from her person to assume the air of a lady of leisure. Wearing it to open the back door was fine because that would indicate the callers were either family, close friends or tradesmen, and they needed to know that work was in progress. Even now, if people arrive when I'm cooking in one of those stripy aprons from Habitat, I still feel a twinge of my mother's disapproval at my complete disregard for apron etiquette.

I have a fondness for many of these old ways. They indicate a detailed attention to social niceties that are falling away in our hectic times. It is surely a good thing for neighbours to show respect for the grief of others, and though I'm not suggesting that there is any less heartache felt by mourners who turn up in jeans and trainers, there is something seemly in giving people's last rite of passage some final dignity. That's why the Devonshire photograph with its old-world deference and paternalist tradition has such an impact.

Sometimes old places survive, too. I don't mean the numerous worthy buildings of architectural merit listed by Heritage experts. I mean the chance survival of somewhere that has by accident somehow escaped the thrust of modern times. I was in Spain recently, driving around the lovely countryside of the north-east. Way back in the 1950s I had arrived there, travelling by train to Barcelona, then taking a bus northwards towards the French frontier. On impulse we decided to stop off at a tiny sandy bay called Llafranc, whose sole attractions were a beachside hotel or two and a few houses and boats. It was idyllic. I had not returned since.

I had long assumed that it had succumbed to the development blight that engulfed the Costa Brava throughout the 1960s. I was wrong. Today Llafranc is a thriving little resort. The sandy road that edged the sea has been tarmacked, and there is a modest spread of holiday apartments. But there are no high rises, no through traffic. The beach is still open and golden. As I idled away an hour or two, I felt as though I was stepping through a time barrier. I dredged my memory to recall how it was – which hotels were where, what cafés we had visited – and came up against my younger self, full of hopes and dreams, with no cares, little money, bags of optimism and an entire future ahead of me. It is hard to believe that fifty years have passed. Sometimes those moments catch us unawares, and prompt a wrenching nostalgia. So it was in Llafranc. So it was with the Devonshire aprons.

~

'WOW!' EXCLAIMED MY GRANDSON. 'You've got one of those! Cool!' What I have is a turntable that plays vinyl records, stacked along with the tape deck, CD and radio player that make up my twelve-year-old sound system. He is impressed. How does it work? I reveal the wonders of needles, grooved tracks and two-sided recordings to someone for whom all this is all completely new. And cool, as is the collection of vinyl recordings in their cardboard covers, fraying at the corners. This turntable plays not only at 33 rpm but also at 45 for my collection of seven-inch records, wonderful songs from Peggy Lee, Edith Piaf and Kiri te Kanawa singing Gershwin. I'm only sad to have mislaid that small plastic disc for those seven-inch recordings that, oddly, had a two-inch centre. That means much of my Bob Dylan and the original music from *The Magic Roundabout* goes unplayed. Sad.*

It is even sadder the next day when the man from Bang & Olufsen comes to check it all out. He has an entirely different take to my grandson. 'Oh, goodness, you still have one of those.' (He of course is in the business of selling me the hugely expensive modern version.) He tells me it's now impossible to buy replacement needles and that, when years ago they announced that they would be discontinuing them, the price shot up amid the general scramble to stock up quickly before supplies ran out. I, not knowing all this, am left with my one single and cherished needle.

*When this article appeared in the *Guardian*, readers sent me as many as fifty of those little discs. A clutch of them now sit in a dish by the record player.

We were taught about built-in obsolescence at school. It was the way economies were structured, so that technical innovation could make its way in the marketplace, driving out the old and decrepit goods that people clung to in their ignorance, and thus keep the wheels turning of productivity, with all its hangers-on in marketing, advertising and such. Needless to say, the truth is that new goods aren't always improved goods. I'm told that vinyl recordings are now valued and collected once again. I could, at moments of redecorating over the decades, so easily have chucked all mine away. How thankful I am that I didn't, and I treat that remaining needle with particular care. Now the word is that the CD is over. Not here it isn't. Beware people proclaiming new and improved ways of doing what was perfectly satisfactory already. They are usually trying to sell you something you don't need.

My kitchen is another treasure trove of the supposedly out of date, including an old egg whisk, tatty and stained – the sort of thing a kitchen-themed pub would have on the wall – and the classic Victorian lemon squeezer. I defy any designer – and that includes Philippe Starck – to design a better way of getting juice out of a lemon than the old-fashioned glass dish with its ridged cone. Sometimes the best design is the first. So what shall I be wearing to the opening of the first Jean Muir shop? Will it be the two-year-old trousers and top, or the fifteen-year-old little blue dress? Neither will look out of fashion. Timeless elegance remains just that. It disproves the fashionistas' advice that says if you haven't worn it for a year, throw it out. I say, keep hold and you won't be sorry.

Taking the issue beyond the trivia of my own life, I think it's time inbuilt obsolescence was rethought. With global problems created by environmental damage and disparate wealth now so compelling, we need to hold on longer to what we have. Why throw away perfectly good and functioning possessions simply because the frenetic world of consumerism pressures you to do so? If every household held on to its white goods one year longer, the landfill problem would ease. If people delayed updating their car we might start to slow down that accelerating drive in the Western world to consume ever more. Given that such decisions would save us money, we could then afford to buy better-quality goods next time, which in turn would last longer.

The rise of the car boot sale, the trade in second-hand clothes, the flourishing of shops such as Curtain Exchange and Oxfam, bear witness to the abundance of things discarded long before their use is ended. I know networks of families with young children who regularly swap clothes between them as one particular size is outgrown by one that is just the right fit for another. My mother, who would never buy antiques because 'you don't know where they've been', would not have approved. But her thinking has gone, along with her generation. Now we can swap and hand down, buy second-hand and used, without that furtive feeling of doing something not quite nice. Which reminds me, where did I put those Biba boots? My daughter might be interested.

~

ADMIT IT. We never thought she could do it. Not in a million years could a wispy Australian actress begin to conjure one of the greatest Hollywood icons of all time. Yet here she is with an 2004 Oscar nomination for her part as Katharine Hepburn in *The Aviator*. OK, so Cate Blanchett has admirable acting skills; her performance as the young queen in the film *Elizabeth* grew from winsome girl to thoughtful monarch with great panache. But then we weren't personally witness to the real-life Elizabeth's quirks and mannerisms, the swoop of her cadences, the bray of her laughter. There was scope for imagination, historical guesswork. There is no guesswork where Katharine Hepburn is concerned. Consider just how familiar we are with Hepburn's wild and wonderful personality. Take the voice alone, a uniquely recognizable drawl, confected partly from her affluent Connecticut background, spiced with an upfront no-nonsense directness of speech. Then there's the appearance: razor slim, looking great in what were then called slacks, her cascades of unruly auburn hair owing nothing to Hollywood bangs and pageboys; and a mouth, wide and mobile, as quick to tease as to rebuke, an ever-moving expressive Pagliacci of a mouth. How would Blanchett – said to have been second choice for the part to Nicole Kidman – manage it?

The answer earned her a well-deserved Oscar for best supporting actress. Impersonation was only part of her triumph. Yes, the drawl is there and the swing of the head. But, more than that, Blanchett somehow seems to inhabit the Hepburn persona, even for those who are devoted to her. For women of a certain age, Hepburn played out in numerous ways how we fantasized our lives could be, with ourselves as bold, successful, challenging women.

First she pulled off the almost impossible trick of being highly individual and resolutely her own woman, while sustaining a career at the heart of the most conformist and clichéd Hollywood years. She was tall where the others were small; flat-chested in an age of jutting breasts; gaunt in her beauty where the studios liked them with chubby cheeks and pert little mouths. Then, she gave every appearance of setting her own agenda, of being in control of her career. The fact that this wasn't strictly the case is evident in a string of duff studio movies that disappeared without trace or regret. We remember only the greats.

What mattered most was that Hepburn played strong women, challenging the male world with talent and wit. Worthies like Marie Curie or goody-goodies like Florence Nightingale were all very well, but we wanted modern heroines with a crisp put-down for condescending men and a way of winning while remaining feminine. Oddly, given the Oscar nominations, one of Hepburn's first films was *Christopher Strong*, where she played the first woman to fly around the world. It set the pattern. In *Morning Glory* she was an ambitious young actress who, surveying the portraits of Ethel Barrymore and Sarah Bernhardt, declares: 'I shall never be wonderful like them ... but I have something wonderful inside me!' She came to outshine them both.

It was in the string of films she made with Spencer Tracy that she acted out the conflicts and dilemmas we were destined to replay in our own lives. Their first film together, *Woman of the Year*, matched a female political pundit with a sports columnist whose marriage is fraught with conflict that is only resolved by her dutifully cooking him breakfast. The sexual politics were dodgy but we got the message. Hepburn and Tracy went from strength to strength. In *Adam's Rib*, they played opposing lawyers, she defending a woman for shooting her unfaithful husband. The script is full of wit, the subtext of their own romance self-evident. In *Pat and Mike* – he the suspect sports promoter, she the all-round sportswoman – again it is a battle of equals, told with love and laughter. How gratifying to learn years later of their twenty-five-year-long love affair, sustained by her loyalty and love despite his being married, a drunk and a Catholic. No wonder their comic timing was so good.

All these films were as emotionally educative for me as the novels *Jane Eyre* or *Middlemarch*. Their good humour suggested that, even as the solemn tomes of feminism dropped on the desk, we should address life's heavy issues with a light heart. Hepburn went on making films – and winning Oscars – into a distinguished old age, and we went on loving her, but her role in helping shape women's idea of themselves eventually passed to others. Now she is portrayed in *The Aviator* as the sometime lover of Howard Hughes. Nothing more. No hint of her Hollywood status or her place in film history. None the less Cate Blanchett's performance deserves an Oscar for bringing that Hepburn spirit back into our lives.

~

SOME THINGS THE old have in abundance, a plenitude of blessings denied to any other age group: memories. Looking back over a life lived long is something we oldies all do, something that brings with it a world of different emotions. Nostalgia is just the start of it; it can open the floodgates to sadness, laughter, remorse, regret, tenderness. We can live whole worlds in our heads, worlds that were ours and remain with us. These are places the young can go to only through archive documentaries and history books, and somehow they never get it quite right. It's never quite as it was for us.

Writing my autobiography involved dredging up much from the past. Happily I have always been a hoarder and the evidence has been first-hand: shoeboxes of letters, throbbing, repetitive love letters, nagging letters from parents. Also a trove of letters that my mother and father wrote to each other, decorous but devoted. And, even more yellowing and frayed than the rest, and thinly spread across the years, a few flimsy missives between my grandparents, usually worrying about money, the payments of modest sums, or accounts of visits to hospitals. Troubles got told in letters.

Later came the photographic record, small sepia snaps catching the folly of young girls in flapper dresses, their young men in plus fours or leaning against motorbikes. My own life makes its appearance in polyphotos, those sheets of tiny square pictures so popular in the 1940s. Most of my growing up is recorded in black and white. Only in the 1960s did we go into colour, and even then we were sparing in our use of film. It was special and costly. One shot of each subject had to suffice. Now people click away recklessly, trusting in sheer numbers to capture one significant image, the story we want the record to tell.

How much are our memories shaped by the evidence that remains, how much distorted? Didn't we always imagine that bowler hats were exclusively the dress of City gents? Yet a letter of my father's tells of how on the day they completed their apprenticeship he and his mates went out and bought themselves bowlers. I have a slew of invitations to sherry parties that recall with a certain fustian nostalgia the mood of my days in 1950s Cambridge. Who now would believe that sherry was the student drink of choice? Thus do archive and memory interweave, adjusting, correcting, renewing. Without the hoard, my memories would be mere fiction.

I am put in mind of all this because my son has just turned forty. (You're really old when it occurs to you to ask your children to lie about their age.) By way of celebration we compiled an album of every year of his life. Here is the hippie child of 1960s parents with shoulder-length hair and a toddler-size afghan coat. Here is the schoolboy daringly sporting flared trousers, fashionable for the first time round in the 1970s. Here are my daughter's first experiments with coloured hair: screaming yellow, then flaming red, once the trendiest way to wind us up. Today using hair colourant is as routine as toothpaste.

We all know the treachery of photography: that it tells a contrived and selected story. But at least it furnishes a way into the past. What the younger generations don't have are letters. They have given up on the written and posted word. Why bother when you can e-mail or phone or text? As we contact each other more often, respond instantly, fill the air with the buzz of perpetual chatter, there is, oddly, nothing to show for it. What record will we leave behind, except for some remote traces on ageing hard drives only to be scavenged by the state police when we come under suspicion?

What will historians and biographers do without letters? Think of the revealing intimacies of Charlotte Brontë to Mrs Gaskell, the shining letters of Keats, the gossip of the Goncourt brothers. Would the record be the same without those poignant despatches from soldiers in the trenches, or the accounts sent home by employees of the East India Company as well as those of the young women travelling to India to become their wives? As the air quivers with the miracles of modern technology and ever new ways of being in touch, I feel a fondness for the handwritten sheet of thoughts and sentiments, the personality of the pen coiling its way across the page. I have my hoard of letters. And I have my memories.

~

I ALREADY HAVE AN IDENTITY CARD. I have it right here: a folded piece of green card, declaring on the cover 'National Registration'. Inside, a National Registration Office stamp tells me it was issued on 15 July 1950. The date is a bit of a mystery: neither a significant birthday – neither eighteen or twenty-one – nor a landmark national crisis. There had been many such documents in the early months of the war and people got used to peremptory orders concerning ration books for food – an allowance of points – and for clothing – a matter of coupons. Everyone had to register with a butcher and a grocer, and they became their single authorized supplier. Faced with war, the population were meekly agreeable to any amount of government regulation.

By 1950, the war had been over for five years yet my identity card has all the harshness of wartime diktats. 'Always carry your identity card. You may be required to produce it on demand by a police officer in uniform or a member of HM Armed Forces in uniform on duty … Any breach of these requirments is an offence punishable by a fine or imprisonment or both.' And within the green folded card is my identity number: LEXJ 259:3. The 3 was because I, the first-born, came after my parents. My father was 1, of course. This number had been drummed into me so thoroughly during the war that it has stayed with me over fifty years later along with that other vital number: the Co-op 'divi'. Ours was 929 and without it we couldn't claim our quarterly dividend. I sense that if I were ever under torture these are the numbers I would struggle to conceal, so deeply is their importance etched in my mind.

Thus it was in wartime that an entire generation came to accept government regulation on a scale never experienced before or since. What's more it was welcomed as a great improvement on the shortages of the First World War. Rationing was seen as conspicuous fairness: the rich and the poor treated as equals. Even the royal family was included. And there was a unanimity then that made us ready to be compliant. We had such a sense of national identity – Britain standing proudly alone against the enemy – that our individual identities, set out in those green cards, were just a part of the greater national identity to which we all belonged. That is no longer the case. The comeback of the identity card coincides with a time of identity crisis. It's said we don't really know who we are any more. We're a more fragmented country, more conscious of our differences than aware, as we once were, of what we have in common.

What's more, government control of our lives, rather than falling away after the war, has become ever more intrusive and all-powerful. Identity cards were finally abolished in 1952 after an incident when a police constable stopped a motorist and asked to see his papers there and then, by the kerbside. The motorist refused and was charged, but a judge later ruled that the police should not demand identity papers as a matter of routine. Does that ruling still stand, I wonder, and will it apply if Tony Blair has his way?

It isn't surprising that we aren't as submissive as once we were. There was a time when you could build a garden shed, park a car or smack a child with that confident sense of identity, of being in charge of your own destiny, that has been so consistently whittled away by the world in which we live. I wonder whether the ID card is a step too far: too intrusive, too Orwellian to be acceptable. Or are people once again, as in wartime, so fearful that they are willing to accept its return? The 1940s was an era of genuine, actual fear, of a proximate and visible enemy. But now people whose lives are in fact less directly threatened than they were then are being encouraged to see the world as perpetually menacing. The prominence given to crime – so-called scroungers, illegal immigrants, lone stalkers, above all the suggestion of ever-present terrorists – winds us up into a state of permanent anxiety, convinced that we live in times of unique terror, rather than in one of the most peace-loving nations on earth.

Personally, having had an identity card once, I would not be much bothered in having to carry one again. What does worry me is the fact that I am constantly losing things: gloves, rail tickets, scarves. I'm sure to lose the new plastic ID. Perhaps it would be better to tattoo the number on my wrist. I'm not serious, of course. Yet I can imagine there's someone somewhere even now thinking up such a notion, some young stripling of an apparatchik, too young and too ignorant to know what resonances that has for those who remember the Holocaust.

~

A NEW RESIDENT HAS ARRIVED in the neighbourhood. She has friends here already so they offer drinks in the square to introduce her, evidence that London's growing sense of community isn't simply an urban myth. She – not long widowed – has downsized from a house to a flat; she moved in three days previously and threw tons of stuff away in the course of the move. Considering how traumatic that must have been, she looks remarkably buoyant. Happily she also has a high-powered job. Two days later she flew to New York.

All of which set me thinking. Looking around the gathered neighbours, I realized that there is only one family who have been here as long as I have. I have lived in the same house for over forty years, moving in, pregnant, in 1963. I am, I surmise, the oldest living inhabitant. This prompts a certain wistfulness. If this were a country village I would no doubt sit in the corner of the snug, sipping port and lemon, chewing my gums and regretting the passing of Old England. But Primrose Hill now thinks of itself as a London village, which is quite a different matter. Here we foregather at pavement coffee shops to talk of current matters – books, plays, parking regulations, Iraq – and only occasionally is anyone interested in how it once was.

We moved in because our family was getting bigger, we had not only a second child, but also an au pair. The essential consideration was space, it didn't matter how run-down. The public gardens in front of the house were cordoned off by gnarled wire netting rather than railings, and were a dumping ground for broken prams and discarded furniture. Worse, the house sat beside a through-road, a rat-run favoured by lorries. Worst of all, Euston station, lurking just behind the tidy streets, still harboured steam trains, filling the air and our curtains with soot. Until recently there were two old biddies (well, about my age, I suppose) who remembered when sheep were grazed in the square. Yes, things have definitely changed.

Will I live out my days here, I wonder, or will I too downsize? Certainly there is little chance of my handing on the family home to the next generation. It doesn't happen like that these days. Only aristocrats – poor things – lumber their eldest sons with dry rot, too many bedrooms and not enough heating. It must be a terrible burden, often bravely borne, so the rest of us can enjoy their architectural heritage.

The problem for me and many like me, living in far more space than we actually need, is that our capital is tied up in our homes and we somehow feel we shouldn't be forced to sell in order to finance our old age. Once the pension provision was enough, yet increasingly the pension shortfall now makes selling inevitable for many. And still we don't want to move. Not only does the house echo with memories of lives lived to the full, the parties of yesteryear, the noisy times of toddlers and teenagers, but we have settled into our furniture and our comfort, and we like it as it is. Outside, too, we know where we are although the scene may have changed: cafés and restaurants thrive where once there was a butcher, a baker and a cobbler. It would not surprise me to learn that those forced to sell, who opt to move from town to country, or abandon a familiar and friendly neighbourhood for a place of strangers, suffer a real sense of loss, possibly even depression.

The country's housing stock is low. Old people are sitting in properties that are too big for them, yet what can motivate them to move on? As we get older it may become imperative. One day I may not be able to manage the stairs. Perhaps for some, their garden becomes a burden to care for and they worry about it. Yet they stay put. For the old, the prospect of such a change is not necessarily the exhilarating adventure it is for the young. I know it will be a great wrench whenever I have to get round to it. If today's architects were to turn their imaginations to sheltered housing I might be interested. How about loft conversions, riverside apartments, granny flats all glass and chrome? The old don't want to be dumped in homes no one else wants. They need light and colour and even style to keep them in touch with the world around them. The great Brazilian architect Oscar Niemeyer is ninety-six years old and said to be still working. Perhaps he has the answer.

~

I HAVE A GROWING AWARENESS that more and more of my life is turning up in museums. It began many years ago when I first visited the Museum of Childhood and was swept back to my early years by babyclothes from the 1930s that were exactly like those in which I watched my mother dress my baby sister. No mother would consider them now; they belong to an era before disposable nappies, before Velcro, before plastic, before nylon. They involved giant safety pins, lots of ribbons and long strips of flannel known as binders, which were wrapped tightly around the baby's belly button. The matter of childbirth was seen as a medical condition. As well as the mother being made to stay in bed upwards of a week afterwards, the baby's navel was treated as an open wound to be poulticed out of sight. Nappies came in two layers: the muslin sheets known as Harrington squares and, over them, the looser one of folded towelling. Despite the effort, everything still got wet, including the bedding, where only a thick and brittle kind of mackintosh protected the mattress. Everything had to be washed, every day. Motherhood was slavery.

Then the Imperial War Museum put on show 'The Forties House', the realistically created two-up, two-down semi which flourished between the wars and was the subject of a Channel 4 series. Welcome home, Joan! I walked in as if expecting to be met by the smell of overcooked cabbage, the burning of toast on the gas grill and the voice of Alvar Liddell coming from the walnut veneer radio. Here it all was: the three-piece suite, the chenille tablecloth, the fringed lampshades and the rag rug. Upstairs were pink satin bedspreads and plump eiderdowns, which, over the years, have somehow transmogrified into duvets. In the kitchen a mangle, a whistling kettle and aluminium saucepans. It was as though a slice had been cut into my memory and a segment made real.

Next time, at the same museum, we visited the Blitz experience. Sitting in the reconstructed air-raid shelter, I reminisced about how, without the spiders and the smell, not to mention the fear, it didn't feel right. Younger generations queued, and shuffled through, falling silent as the sound effects overwhelmed. Yet I couldn't help feeling that, although the bric-a-brac was genuine enough and the period research impeccable, the actual experience was missing. This is not the fault of the museums. You can't re-create how other people experienced earlier times. You can, however, have a pretty good stab at it, and all credit to the Imperial War Museum for trying.

I had another chance in 2005 at trying to conjure up the past, this time with Coleridge and Wordsworth. I joined them, for a Radio 4 programme, at a magical moment in their lives when they came together as young men with an idea to make money, get famous, and have a wonderful time in the process. First I was at Coleridge's cottage in Nether Stowey from where he and the Wordsworths – William and his sister Dorothy – set out on a walk one November day in 1787, planning to write a poem as they walked and sell it for £5. That poem became 'The Rime of the Ancient Mariner'; the book that followed became *Lyrical Ballads*, anonymously published but none the less destined to make their names.

Then I was at Alfoxden House, in the panelled room where it is said Coleridge first read the 'Ancient Mariner' aloud to his friends. I fell to wondering again how much one can recapture the past. What are we seeking when we half close our eyes and imagine the burr of Coleridge's West Country voice rolling out before his spellbound listeners? Coleridge describes the Nether Stowey cottage as 'a hovel', 'a shed', damp and infested with mice. It is nothing like that now. It is decorous and clean, with period chairs set out to please the modern eye. What must have been a rumbustious and noisy household, full of argumentative friends distrusted by the locals for their radical opinions, is now tastefully silent awaiting its awed visitors. Only in the tangled garden behind the house did I catch a glimpse of what Coleridge might have known.

Despite such obvious incongruities, museums now draw us in ever-increasing numbers with expectations of discovering how it once was. Every half-term, Britain's museums swarm with families. You can hardly move at the Natural History Museum, the Science Museum, the Maritime Museum, for children tugging at generous parents to come-see-this, let's-try-that. And the museums are ready for them, planning, designing and presenting ever more engaging exhibitions. I know because in 2005 I served on the jury for the Gulbenkian Prize, the country's largest cultural prize – £100,000 – that goes to the Museum of the Year. We toured the country surveying the great range of competitors, from the high-tech brilliance of Birmingham's Thinktank science museum, to Black History Month at Sutton House, Hackney; from Reticulum at the Museum of Antiquities in Newcastle, to a touring exhibition of Romany history in Pembrokeshire. Everywhere these displays are feeding what seems an insatiable appetite to know more. Perhaps it's all those quizzes on television that have done it: knowledge being worth while simply for its own sake. Certainly today's young people know more than we ever did about the artefacts and circumstances of how life used to be, how it still is and how it might become.

As with all success stories, demand races ahead of the capacity to meet it: never enough seats for a hit show, never sufficient tickets for a football final. In the two years that followed the government's free-admissions policy, begun in 2001, there were almost 11 million extra museum visitors. Figures had doubled to 13.3 million compared to 7.7 million the previous year. Attendances at the Science Museum rose by a dramatic 120 per cent. The numbers are staggering. That's why museum leaders from all sectors – national, regional and independent – are constantly seeking further funds. In recent pleas to government they have asked for an extra £115 million a year to meet the massive demands of popularity. This is, after all, education by another route, one that children are eager to enjoy.

For me, I simply throw open my cupboards and survey the debris of decades lurking there – the 1940s gas mask, the 1960s pressure cooker, the 1970s coffee percolator. One day, perhaps – via a car boot sale at the end of the world – some of it might even go on show.

~

MOST OF THE THINGS THAT I DO, as the years go by, I do less often, but I take greater pleasure in each occasion, whether it's listening to a Schubert quintet or relishing the subtle flavours of a zesty marmalade. But one thing I am doing more and more, both with pleasure but unavoidably with distress: I turn each day with fearful anticipation to the obituary pages of the newspapers and find there people who have meant something to me.

There is not a week goes by now without the death of someone who may have been an acquaintance, even a real friend, or simply someone whose work and life has been significant in my own. I sense that, even as I rustle the turning pages, I am steeling myself against what I might find there, and how I might respond. When I was younger it was with a cry of surprise, even outrage. The fact is that the people one knows, friends, of course, but even acquaintances or those who move in the same worlds, are for the majority around one's own age. And here in my forties and fifties would be the record of early and unexpected deaths. It was natural to be ambushed by sudden and raw grief.

There is less surprise now. Instead I have a sense of mellow resignation as to how things must be, a recognition that we are all passing this way and that, to name recent losses, the novelist Bernice Rubens or the poet Thom Gunn have simply arrived there before me. Something like a long low sigh overwhelms me, I look up at the winter sky, as I did each evening as my sister lay dying, and I think again how frail we all are in face of the power and remorselessness of elemental nature. No thought is more appropriate in these sorrowful times.

Yet whereas I once read the untimely obituary with a sense of injustice and a brisk anger at death, I am now coming almost to enjoy them. If journalism is the first draft of history, then obituaries are the first entries in the *Oxford Dictionary of National Biography*. They are usually a surprisingly good read, and often more insightful than a routine magazine or newspaper profile might be. There is the fascination of discovering so much you hadn't known before, at the moment of realizing that you can now never speak of it together. I would have enjoyed talking to Bernice Rubens about her Welsh background. The chance has gone. I was amazed to learn that Anthony Sampson came from a family of scientists. Had I known, it might have figured in one of our interviews. The opportunity has passed.

Such personal reactions come largely from the pattern of my working life. But what we can all see in obituaries are the numerous and even devious ways people arrived at their achievements. The trajectories of lives are so various. Some have to escape the clutches of large and dominating families; others rejoice in them. Many owe much to inspiring teachers pointing the way; others, lacking such advice, make false starts. Some pursue planned careers with single-minded dedication. Others move apparently without direction in life before seizing on a role that fits them like a glove. I read with amusement and some scepticism Humphrey Carpenter's reported account of not making it in television. He was, of course, a consummate radio broadcaster and a hugely successful writer. We can see now that any television success would have deprived us of his many fine biographies.

Then there are the pictures, so often a treasure trove of period photography: the staged theatre still, the film star in his prime, the artist at his easel. How good it was to see Margaret Gardiner, who died in 2005 at the age of one hundred, standing beside what looks like a Barbara Hepworth, precisely as so many of us remember her, shaggy but stylish, her face exactly as described by Janet Morgan who wrote the obituary, as being 'like a friendly cat's, intelligent and eager'. This is an arena of journalism that goes unsung. There are no awards; attention focuses on the subject, not the writer. And once the heightened awareness of loss passes, the obituaries themselves lose their immediacy and warmth of feeling. When they are collected in anthologies and on the internet, the tenderness of felt loss goes cold and they shift from topical poignancy to become documents of record. The grand names will live on in the pantheon of history, but most of us pass from the fond recollections of friends into the annals of family lore, leaving perhaps a small footnote of interest only to our descendants. *Sic transit* . . .

PART THREE

Tomorrow

'Grow Old along with me!
The best is yet to be,
The last of lie, for which the first was made.'

ROBERT BROWNING

EIGHT

Today's World

GETTING OLDER IS like walking further into a forest where suddenly all the vegetation has changed and keeps on changing, the leaf and bole of springtime yielding to alien and fantastical shapes, distorted growths and unexpected contusions. It is hard to imagine that this is the same forest, the same life, that we set out on so many years ago. It is not simply a matter of technology. We always expected that to change, and if it proceeds in a linear fashion there's nothing too startling about it. Recorded music once came from shellac records on wind-up gramophones and it now comes downloaded into iPods. I can understand that.

It's the unexpected sidestepping developments that are so unsettling. Who would once have imagined that people would eat so many of their meals away from home, even in the street? Who would believe people would fly from one side of the world to another for a weekend break? Who would expect affluent people in such large numbers to be taking substances that render them insensible? On a wider canvas, how strange that empires now seem to rise and fall so swiftly. The British empire lasted for some two hundred years, the Russian for a mere seventy. The USA's hegemony is already being challenged, while India and China seem to be galloping to overtake all three of them as the world's booming economies. We could have predicted that warfare would be transformed by developments in atomic physics but not by the far more insidious impact of the suicide bomber. The planet's problems, whether it's Aids or global warming, are at our door, in our newpapers and on television, in a global glut of information which has characterized the last few decades. That's a sensational range of changes to have lived through in one lifetime. It's impossible to keep up with the spirit of the age. It is racing away from us into an unimaginable future.

Except for one circumstance. The rapidly increasing number of the old in the populations of the West may itself come to define some aspects of how society develops. The demographic divide between the ageing nations and the countries with populations mostly under thirty will have consequences we can't imagine. The pressure on resources, not just oil but water and food, will direct policies we can't conceive. We may ourselves be an important part of how the future shapes up. Here are a few home thoughts on such matters, garnered over the two years up to 2006.

~

WHY AREN'T I MORE AFRAID? The terror stakes are clearly ratcheting up daily. If it isn't a case of terrorist alarums, spying conspiracies and intensifying international tensions, then it's a domestic agenda of paedophile infiltration, health-bug alerts and escalating street violence. Feel afraid, feel very afraid. Why don't I?

Spike Milligan had the right idea when he wrote:

Things that go 'bump' in the night
Should not really give one a fright.
It's the hole in each ear
That lets in the fear,
That, and the absence of light!

It is now completely impossible to get a hold on what degree of threat actually exists, but the ears let in plenty of troublesome noise that makes us uneasy, without any compensating light. I'm therefore trying to assess today's risks against others I've known.

I was right to be afraid during the war against Hitler because he made his intentions very clear, dropping bombs near where I lived and setting fire to the homes of my school friends. I threw a frantic tantrum of fear early one evening when I saw my father take a rifle from a cupboard and head out into the night. My imagination told me he would be killed and lost to me for ever. In fact he was going to Home Guard practice with the local equivalent of *Dad's Army*'s Mr Mainwaring. Fear, rightly felt, but inappropriately applied.

It was in the late 1950s and early 1960s when I felt real fear again. In the race for power, America and China were both testing nuclear bombs above ground, pouring contamination directly into the atmosphere. In 1957 there were forty-two above-ground nuclear explosions around the globe. Soon deadly strontium 90 was in the milk that we were giving children, and I had a small daughter. That same year there was a major nuclear accident at Windscale that released radioactive material into the skies above Britain. The discharge of pollution went on for five days, driving up radioactivity to ten times the normal level. CND was founded then and there to address those real and present dangers and without it the arms race and international rivalries would have gone unchallenged. By the Easter of 1960 I was joining the Aldermaston marchers in Trafalgar Square. Then, as now, we were right to be fearful of nuclear pollution and nuclear weapons. The idea that Britain is planning a whole new generation of 'nukes' causes me real alarm. I am much more afraid of arms manufacturers than I am of fanatical clerics.

The really big fear came in 1962 and had all of my generation in its grip. The occasion, referred to now as 'the Cuban Missile crisis', takes its place coolly in the pages of history as a pivotal moment in the Cold War between East and West. At the time it felt red-hot. Khrushchev had installed nuclear warheads in Cuba, supposedly on America's doorstep, and Kennedy challenged him to back down. Nuclear war was imminent. We lived in dread from minute to minute. I recall flashlight photography taking place in the office next to mine and someone starting in alarm: was this the first nuclear flash then? In those days we had been given daft civil defence advice about putting brown paper bags on our heads and getting under the table. America, in contrast, had provided itself with loads of nuclear shelters. We knew we weren't getting the full story, even then.

And now? Perhaps age makes one less fearful of catastrophe. I fear for my family more than I do for myself. They've been told that, if London is suddenly nuked, they are not to come looking for me, but to hunker down and see to their own survival. This is not brave but realistic. Terrorism, after all, is a technique of conflict, not the conflict itself. And just as we can't uninvent nuclear weapons, we can't eliminate the idea of terrorism from the human psyche. It will always be there to tempt the disaffected, the extremist, the mentally disturbed and the power-mad. So from now on it will always be part of our lives. The idea of winning a war on terror is a political conceit of the unsophisticated mind. Meanwhile a million people worldwide will die each year as a result of road accidents. How about the car as a weapon of mass destruction? How fearful should we be of going for a spin?

~

IS THIS IT THEN, global warming, has it finally arrived? Have the advance publicity, the dire warnings, the environmental polemics finally come to this: a sequence of days so blisteringly hot that the sweat is dripping onto the keyboard, the ice tray has to be constantly replenished, the windows thrown wide at the cool extremities of the day, while in the meantime curtains, shutters and blinds must be closed as for noontide in the Mediterranean?

I grew up at a time when vexatious weather was a given, and as we lived near Manchester, that 'given' usually meant rain. We studied world climates as though they were permanent fixtures, the Sahara an aberrant stretch of sand, the Amazon forest an eternal and inviolable spread of green. Rivers rose and fell, so we learnt about estuaries and deltas. Mountain ranges wore a coat of perpetual snow, as did the poles where recklessly brave individuals would battle the elements for national glory. But we expected those elements to stay the same.

Not that we didn't experience extremes of weather. The winter of 1947 was exceptionally hard. Every box Brownie in the land recorded the depth of snowfalls, Mum and Dad wielding spades to dig out the garden gate and even, if you had one, the precious car. Ink froze in the inkwells, there was no central heating. But there were compensations. Local pools froze solid and everyone took to their skates. At Oxford people skated along the river; at Windsor you could cross the Thames on a bicycle. In the school playground we polished tracks of ice to a glasslike finish and then slid along them at a frantic pace. Laughter rose bright and brittle in the crisp air.

A decade later I recall pea-soupers, grey-green fogs so dense you struggled to see your hand in front of your face. In 1952 there was a four-day pea-souper that it is claimed killed 4,000 Londoners. I remember that in the mid-1950s we had somehow got ourselves to Sadler's Wells and when our bus home found itself on the pavement and up against a shop window, we knew it was time to disembark and grope our own way back to Hampstead. In 1956 the Clean Air Act imposed smokeless zones on inner cities, sulphur dioxide was reduced and we began to see the sky.

Such brief episodes of exceptional weather were considered just that: exceptional. Not any more. Now what is happening is seen as part of a bigger story: relentless climate change at an accelerating rate. We're told there has been more alteration in the condition of the earth in the last twenty years than in the last two hundred, and in the last two hundred more than in the previous two thousand. As the experts roll out the numerous ways that we're all going to have to adjust, I can see that being older has its advantages.

There's bound to be a big push against those ghastly 4 x 4 cars. But I don't have to transport children any more, and the macho image does me no favours. I might even swap my Toyota Celica for the electric and petrol hybrid Toyota Prius. The era of cheap airfares will come to an end, but the old seem to prefer cruises. With my hybrid vehicle I won't have a guilty conscience about idling my way across Europe. Travelling more slowly may come back into fashion. Cities will have to have designated cycle lanes before I venture out on a bicycle, but I'm well aware that walking further would help keep me nimble. Perhaps it's time to try the pilgrims' path to Santiago de Compostela. Otherwise, in Britain, there's the senior railcard and the freedom pass. I quite enjoy chatting to the stallholders at the local farmers' market, so perhaps I can wean myself off those polished and flawless vegetables flown in from Spain or Israel and buy locally instead. When it comes to downsizing my house, I could well choose somewhere on high ground – away from the floods – and try installing solar energy. Yes, the life changes that come with age will play well with the green agenda.

The psychology's right too. When I was young and eager I wanted to grab and hold as much as I could of what life had to offer. It needed considerable effort and a sense of frantic activity to travel, read, work and play as much as I wanted to. Somehow the urgency of that enthusiasm has waned. Better to enjoy at a slower pace and perhaps a greater depth the pleasures that endure. Old age is about making fewer demands on yourself ... and also, it could be, on the planet.

~

WE ARE TO BE OFFERED CHOICE on every hand. Suddenly choice is the latest political mantra, as though choice will remedy all ills, win votes, make people happy. The evidence of a long life is that it will do none of these things.

How many teenagers have howled in rage at their parents, 'I didn't ask to be born'? They've realized that they've arrived, without any choice, as the children of two given parents, of given intelligence, class and outlook. They may be growing up in Surbiton or Sandringham but they have no choice in the matter. I, as it happens, grew up in Bakewell Road, long before that became my married surname. Bakewell Road, a place of comfy semi-detacheds, was a 'given' in my life. In my imagination I wanted to live either in a small clapboard house in New England, preferably next door to the family in *Little Women*, or somewhere on the high western plains where I could be rescued by John Wayne whenever I was abducted by what we then called Red Indians. I lived out some of these fantasies with my friends in the fields and woods that surrounded our homes. We knew it was never going to be a real option. The choices in your head are never matched by the choices in reality.

Choice as we grew up was between two or three schools, sub-ject to which of them would have us, and then, if we were so inclined, between a few universities, depending on whose stand-ards we had met in exams. Choice, then as now, was limited by what was available. Post-war education policy widened the choic-es for some, so that grammar schools took in children on merit rather than for fees. All along, other children – in Sandringham and similar places – were being privately educated and enjoying small classes, with a curriculum that included the classics, as well as plentiful sports facilities. Money allowed them to exercise more choice. It was how the world was.

I can see it is how the world still works. But everyone pretends that choice – open and free choice – can be made available everywhere and fairly distributed. Choices about education and health are being seen as part of the consumer society, for the good of all, as a matter of lifestyle aspiration. We're beginning to think of them as we think of clothes and cars: get the best you can afford, keep up with the trend, show off what you have, feel good about keeping level with, or just ahead of, your peers. Parents will move house, join churches, anything to get their children into the school of choice, a criterion measured in terms of league tables and pupil behaviour. The government encourages such com-petitiveness, rewarding the best schools with resources to expand. Instead they should treat education and health provision as a stable and continuing part of the public polity, dedicated to maximizing the good for each in the interest of the good of all. How about just making every school good enough so that people can be satisfied, as we were, with the nearest one available?

In medicine, too, the choices are often ones of lifestyle. People pay for private medicine for the sake of a private room and decent carpets on the floor. When it comes to the most up-to-date medical facilities, the NHS is as good as any. Most crucially, what everyone needs and deserves is a good local GP clinic, plus a local hospital that not only offers the services we need but can also refer us to the appropriate consultants. Who needs more choice than that? Grandiose promises of choice can only lead to disappointment. Realistic expectations are a sounder base for a contented electorate.

Being content with what is possible is a neglected virtue. As you get older, you have no option. Choices narrow and you get used to the idea. For me, the body's limitations mean that rock climbing is now out, and for every Indian nonagenarian photographed doing the marathon, there are plenty who would settle for a lounger on a cruise liner. Choices in family life diminish; the children have long flown the nest and may well be pursuing careers in Bangkok or Boston. The death of a partner leaves many with no other choice than to be lonely. People getting by on modest pensions know that the days of carefree holidays or even a company car are long gone. It's called downsizing but it means living on less.

Finally there's the prospect of the eventual move to the care home. How much choice will we be offered there, I wonder? And, when it comes to the end, can we avoid living out our last illness in a bed next to a total stranger of the opposite sex? Such small but significant choices will matter when the time comes. As to the choice of how and why we die, there, of course, we often have no choice at all.

~

IN 2005 A JOB VACANCY occurred for someone in their seventies. It was widely mentioned in the media, amid considerable excitement, but there was no great rush of applicants. The opportunity crops up about every twenty-six years. However, the relevant qualifications aren't the sort of thing you're likely to have on your CV. In fact, DV (*Deo Volente*) would be more appropriate. But let that wait. First I considered the job description: you would head up possibly the largest organization in the world whose mission statement reaches into every country of the globe. You would operate from within what is virtually a principality, based in a palace of sumptuous richness, and you would officiate in surroundings graced with priceless art and artefacts. From here you would travel the world, bearing a message of humility and love to its wretched. It would come within your remit to pronounce, for those in your 'company', on matters of contraceptive practice, especially those that might limit the spread of Aids, on marital relationships, on what you deem to be certain bodily abominations, on scientific developments that could save lives and on the specifics as to how people should meet their death.

In this you would have the unquestioning support of like-minded people, for it would be in your gift to appoint to office only those who shared your views and to marginalize those who disagreed. It would br an awesome responsibility, but you would be answerable to no one on this earth; your reward, which would be guaranteed and go beyond the dreams of men, would be somewhere else entirely. However, for this superhuman role, you would not be expected to have led a blameless life heretofore. Indeed, the first person to hold the office made a serious blunder early on by denying his personal loyalty to the chairman of the company even before cockcrow. Your tenure would only end with your death, which would occasion a media jamboree on an unprecedented level, bringing together the heads of rival organizations that hold entirely different view; to speak of what a force for unity and peace you had been. This irony, of course, reflects badly on them, but not on you, claiming as you do infallibility for your judgements.

The first and most absolute qualification for this job is that you must be male and a virgin. Those who make up your court will be male virgins also, as will those who implement your policies. The same will be true of those who make up your appointments board – indeed, they will even dress as you do now and be similarly tended in domestic and household management by an array of devoted, celibate women. Many other outstanding attributes would of course be expected of you, but unless these first two were in place, there would be no future for your skills. I had thought of applying myself; after all, it's said there was once a Pope Joan, but she came to no good. Giving birth to a child rather gave the game away and she had to be done to death at once.

Another job vacancy arose at the same time in 2005, nearer home, but nothing could be in starker contrast. Here the fallibility of human judgement was up for rigorous assessment. Virtually anyone was eligible to apply, whatever their sex or personal history. Former holders of the post – in a time when the media were less inquisitive – were known to have led rather rackety home lives. It matters more today that you should be able to field a family, a glamorous wife and assorted children, all available for the occasional photoshoot but otherwise kept discreetly in the background. Some candidates leave it late, meeting the family qualification just days before the application date closes. It will play well if you declare allegiance to some religion or other, but not enough to really interfere. Earlier candidates who admitted to being agnostic made it no further than the shortlist.

You will be promised enormous power to change things and you will want to do so, but events will conspire to thwart you. Your colleagues, chosen for their loyalty, will quickly be in uproar at your unilateral decisions and will need to be sacked. Others will have been turned over in the media for practices falling short of absolute probity, and will either be found jobs abroad or will retire until the uproar dies down. You will have made promises you can't keep; your efforts to neutralize your critics will send them to address debates up and down the land. Your mistakes will not be forgiven and will haunt you even after cockcrow. Your tenure will be risky throughout and could end after four years, when your going will be attended with mockery and derision. You may well wish you had applied for the other job. Either way, retirement suddenly looks a whole lot more attractive.

~

I DID WELL FROM THE 2005 BUDGET; it was the eighth in Gordon Brown's reign as Chancellor and before he became the longest-serving incumbent since Gladstone, as he did in the spring of 2006. His has been on the whole a wise and subtle guardianship of the economy. In that year I benefited from a council tax rebate, a higher winter fuel allowance and my children stood to gain from the increased inheritance tax allowance. I was grateful, but thoughtful too. The last of those budget concessions applied primarily to the cosy middle classes. If you have nothing to leave when you die, then where's the benefit?

It was in response to these election pay-outs that I've begun counting the pennies. It was a chastening exercise, when others that I knew were counting their shares. How would it be to live on much, much less? Whichever end of the financial spectrum you are, there comes a time to wonder how the sums will add up. How, as year follows year, will the resources you have, plus those you can claim, affect the lifestyle you're used to?

I had been further prompted by Jamie Oliver's revelation that the sum of money spent by local councils on each child's school lunch was in some cases no more than 37p. Could I possibly manage on so little and still have a healthy diet? And how do those living on the basic pension – no great leap there, I notice – get through the week? The first thing worth noting is that today's old-age pensioners come from a thrifty generation. Habits gained during wartime childhoods remain entrenched. We never throw away leftovers, being adept at turning chicken carcasses into soup and cold roast meats into shepherd's pie. We make a point of switching off electric lights and turning the heating off overnight; we don't swill away a bowlful of hot water when it might serve a second purpose; we empty the teapot on the roses. We probably groom and hang our clothes so they don't lose their shape. We may well be the last generation to use shoe trees. I get two cups of tea from every teabag. Later generations who don't have the thrift habit – who discard and abandon things that are half used – will find it much harder to get by.

Having known life before the packeting and marketing revolutions encased everything in plastic or bonded in it impenetrable wrapping, we know that real value often lies in goods sold naked and unadorned. Consider newspapers: the weekend heavies will last all week and then do service for the cat litter. Consider the joys of browsing for second-hand paperbacks where long-out-of-print gems can be had for a song. Relish the flavour of fresh vegetables – cheap enough to meet the Jamie Oliver challenge, healthy enough to do away with the need for diets and all those proprietary medicines. The pennies are beginning to take care of themselves.

Then it's worth cashing in, so to speak, on all the things the old get for free. No prescription charges for us. Londoners have long had free bus and tube travel. Now its said bus rides are to become free around the country, so nothing can stop us getting to museums, art galleries and libraries, most of them once again provided entirely free. Churches were once free, too, of course, although now you have to pay to get into the posh ones – cathedrals, Westminster Abbey and others. But parish churches don't charge. Indulging an interest in ecclesiastical architecture comes cheap. Most theatres give concessions for senior citizens, though that may limit you to matinée performances, which are, for that reason, usually full of older and attentive audiences.

There's also the money spent to save money: once you've met the initial outlay the benefits mount up. The senior railcard is a blessing. So too are all those membership subscriptions to 'Friends of' organizations. I'm a veteran of the film and television industry: that gives me free access to cinemas, mostly at odd times of day and with the co-operation of the manager. Both the Tate Gallery and the Royal Academy number their memberships over

60,000; once they've paid for membership, all those oldies get in free to as many as six shows a year!

The fact is older people tend to be time rich, cash poor. With their capital tied up in their houses, even those who are apparently well off tend to be thrifty from day to day. But, in their favour, they have time on their hands: time for gardening, which can yield cut flowers for the house throughout the summer; time to walk rather than having to refuel the car; time for long slow cooking that transforms the cheapest cuts into succulent dishes and again meets the Jamie Oliver criterion. So it's not all misery and penny-pinching for the old. There's skill and satisfaction in living on a reasonably tight budget which, thanks to Gordon, is not quite as tight any more.

~

STATISTICS ARE THE raw material of media debate. They sound absolute, finite, the truth incarnate, and among them a particular clutch stick in my mind. Those for average life expectancy in Africa are alarming: Ghana, fifty-seven; Sudan, fifty-six; Nigeria, fifty-one; Ethiopia, forty-seven; Uganda and Somalia, forty-six; Tanzania, forty-three, Zimbabwe and Sierra Leone, thirty-four. And things will get worse in sub-Saharan Africa because of the now extensive HIV infection. We in the developed world can have no idea what it is to live with such a prospect. We who have come to expect our lives to continue well into our eighties have to struggle to imagine living in a world that is losing a generation to Aids. Worldwide, 42 million have already died from Aids, 80 per cent of them in sub-Saharan Africa. There are 15 million Aids orphans, 80 per cent of them in Africa. Many such children are already being brought up by grandparents, having lost both parents to the HIV epidemic. In due course those same children will grow up and have children of their own. Who will be the grandparents to them? In decades to come, sub-Saharan Africa could be facing a generation without grandparents.

Life expectancy in the developed world – Japan's is highest of all – means that a three-generational family is what we expect. We automatically regard grandparents as part of the social and family pattern of our community. We assign them a specific place at the table, and a role in the emotional and psychological evolution of their children and grandchildren. On the broader scale, our culture at large relies on the wisdom and experience of its elders for guidance.

So what are grandparents good for? And what will the young families of Africa miss out on? Certainly it's my experience that women look to their mothers at the time when they are having their own children. It is a visceral tie. Talking of how they themselves came into the world with the very woman who was involved is reassuring, a source of traditional advice and as emotionally bonding as any human relationship can be. It is for this that petty quarrels are put aside, that distances are crossed, that incompatible lifestyles are tolerated. Mothers and daughters matter to each other at such moments.

Grandparents also have more time. Two-job families leave little space for those easygoing times together. Grandparents are good at nursery rhymes – they probably know more, too. They pass on the old wives' tales of yesteryear. They remember mnemonics and their multiplication tables. They enjoy reading and playing games.

They remember their own *Blue Peter* days and can be a dab hand with two toilet rolls and some cotton wool. I'm sure African grandparents had their own equivalent. The relationship between the elder generation and the very young in terms of play and discipline is of a different quality and may be more effective than that governed by the immediate urgencies of parents.

Grandparents are often less anxious. They aren't fuelled by driving ambition for themselves any more. It's all too late for that. So they may well be more relaxed than their children about underachieving youngsters. They are wise to the shallowness of human aspirations and able to take pleasure in things that parents overlook. Grandparents have tales to tell, of what life was like when they were young, before television, before mobile phones, before playstations. In Africa, it may well be before independence, before the civil war, before oil.

Grandparents are vessels for the continuing traditions of the community, although this is not always good news. A group of Ethiopian women in London once explained to me that it was the grannies who sought to perpetuate the tradition of female genital mutilation. As the women campaigned to liberate their own daughters from the custom, it was the grannies they had to defy. Surely this is an extreme and untypical case. Far more typically, grandparents offer to the instability of youth the gravitas of age and skills for successful survival. Their view is long, their outlook benign. Their seriousness redresses the wildness of the young. Grandparents can do much by their personal influence on, and example to, the young to steer the steady direction of a society. What will Africa's young people do without them?

Sometimes there are almost substitutes. Britain's Voluntary Service Overseas – VSO – now takes recruits up to the age of seventy-five. Twenty per cent of their volunteers are over fifty. Apart from the job they do, such people, being part of the community, often befriend local children. That's what John and Ann Tennant did in the Gambia. They went there when John was already in his sixties and soon became popular: 'The children would run into our compound; we had paper, crayons and things. They liked that. Sometimes when we were tired they would be noisy and irritating. But when the time came for us to leave the children said, "We will have a farewell party ... with skipping and games and biscuits."' And so they did. Just as their own grandparents would.

~

AT BRISTOL'S TEMPLE MEADS STATION recently I saw a wonderful sight: a full-size, thoroughly functioning steam train, gearing up to depart the platform where I joined other amazed onlookers to watch what was happening. Railway people said, 'Oh, we do this from time to time; it's nothing special.' Special it most certainly was. As the giant beast lumbered into action, the glisteningly oiled wheels starting their glide forward and the engine let out a fantastic noise: *shoo, shoo, shoo*. Just the sound we had mimicked as children. Then it belched great columns of black smoke into the glass dome of the station building. Suddenly the glamour fell away and I recalled that the noise and the smoke of steam trains were truly a menace, giving us smog, staining our buildings, rotting our curtains and clogging our lungs. The golden age of steam suddenly looked very tarnished.

We glamorize the past at our peril and we neglect its truths to even greater peril. I have recently been coming to the defence of history in a quite practical way. I had only vaguely realized that schoolchildren have the option of dropping all history lessons at the age of fourteen. Currently the Historical Association is gearing up to provide teachers, parents and children themselves with materials that will convince them of the value, benefits and pleasure of studying history. I, among others, have offered testimony that history is essential to an understanding of our lives and our world.

Teaching has been revolutionized since my day. Long gone are the times when we sat in rows of wooden desks in our own classroom, and teachers moved from class to class at a lesson's end. Now, every forty minutes there is total upheaval as the entire school is on the move, resembling nothing more than an airport terminal on a Bank Holiday. Why, I never understand. But there you are ... I'm whingeing about how it was better in my day. It wasn't. I was taught, as was then the tradition, that history was a series of ongoing events that followed on from one another, furnishing us with dates of kings and queens, laws and wars, treaties and revolutions. Only in the case of the latter were we invited to examine why they had happened at all. Revolutions were perceived as nasty irritants that cropped up from time to time, disturbing the smooth flow of events that in themselves have some natural legitimacy. Only slowly did I come to relish the intricacies of cause and effect that make turbulent times such hell to live through and so fascinating to study. One day the coming generation will discover this for themselves when they learn about the Iraq wars. Always supposing that history lessons survive, that is.

How should we connect to our past? First, we are here, the elders of the tribe, living longer with memories reaching back into the past. 'Do you remember the olden days, Grandma?' I was asked by a six-year-old. Well, yes I do. Many of us do. More and more schools are using the recollections of families to set in context events of recent history. I was called on to be someone's homework recently and to offer up anecdotes about the Blitz. I hope the lesson not only enriched the hard facts of dates and battles with colourful homely tales, but also showed how divergent different versions of history can be, how tenuous our sense of what other times were like. How, for example, can one possibly convey the euphoria of those post-war years?

It is hard to describe what optimism feels like when so many are pessimistic. Oh, how we loved the welfare state. How we rejoiced in the National Health Service. How we marvelled at free prescriptions, free doctor's visits, free dentistry; families were relieved of the fear of doctor's bills and the cost of being ill. To those used to not having much, very little can seem like riches indeed. The state took upon itself to provide for all such needs for everyone. Was there ever a more benign philosophy conceived in the interest of all? As we contemplate changes in today's health provision, a history lesson might be necessary in order to understand how we got here from there.

History has shaped Iraq too. Generations of us were given lessons on the collapse of the Ottoman empire, the carve-up among world powers, the rivalry between France and Britain for the oil fields of the Middle East, the international trade-offs early last century that drew the lines on the map that we know today. A few more history lessons among our leaders might give them a finer grasp of what is possible. Certainly history should be a core

'A foolish consistency is the hobgoblin of little minds.'

RALPH WALDO EMERSON

NINE
Attitudes

THERE WAS ONCE a time at the BBC when broadcasters were meant to be neutral. This was during a period when the values of Lord Reith still hung in the air, implicitly understood rather than spelt out too exactly. I recall a BBC contract of the 1960s with a clause hedging me about with conditions as to what and where I could make public my views. In effect, not much and not in many places. It was a clause I always struck out before signing.

Two developments have changed all that. Broadcasters have become swept up in the celebrity culture and now every broadcaster must be a personality. This allows them to sound off about almost everything, daring their employers to sack them. It never happens. So broadcasters declare their views about all and sundry and the clause has presumably long been dropped from BBC contracts.

Having grown to maturity as a journalist in the first era and now living out my life in the second, I find myself liberated. All those opinions I once so assiduously kept to myself have begun to leak out all over the place, and without dire results. I could once have expected to be called before some grey suit of authority and told how I was compromising the BBC's integrity. Not any more: John Humphrys could reveal his most waspish opinions of politicians at a dinner where he was the paid speaker, and the most the BBC could expect was a rather half-hearted expression of regret. The time was when he would have been booted from the front door within hours.

Now my life is full of attitude. I have discovered I have opinions on a whole swathe of issues on which for many broadcasting years I maintained my neutrality. 'What do you think, yourself?' I would be asked after a particularly controversial *Heart of the Matter*. The question always thrilled me. It meant I hadn't shown my hand. Newspapers love the showing of hands. That's what columns are for. So here are a clutch of liberated responses to events around me. A number refer to the election of 2005. That's because I took it very seriously and thought long and hard about how to vote. You'll see why. I was also intrigued by Michael Howard's role, his age and his attempts to appeal to older voters. He didn't appeal to me. Nor did I vote the way I had done consistently for thirty years. It isn't time yet to get stuck in a rut.

~

THE GLASTONBURY FESTIVAL OF 2005 was a particularly rainy
event, but I felt at the time that sticking in the mud may not always
be confined to Glastonbury. Being stuck in the mud of ideas was
what concerned me. It gets easier as you get older. It feels so cosy
to snuggle down with all those old opinions, formulated in the
days when argument was fresh and juicy, when the blood ran hot
with indignation and the heart sang with new hopes. Attitudes
forged in the heat of youth and enthusiasm grow into the
comfortable baggage of middle years and the comforting
certainties of wistful old age. How sure we were that we were right
and isn't history turning out to prove that we were? Didn't we
always agree that 'to jaw-jaw is better than to war-war'? Didn't we
know that inequality breeds resentment, that those without the
means to redress injustice will turn to violence, that to bring
conflict to an end you will have to talk to the enemy? There you
are then. Do as we tell you.

Of course, that's not what happens. History shows that the
wheel has to be reinvented with each generation. Bush ended up
talking to insurgents; Sharon surprised Israel and the world by
making unexpected, if cunning, concessions in Gaza; Mugabe,
once the heroic leader of independent Zimbabwe, surprised
people when he turned tyrant. I find it hard not to sit back smugly
with the ragbag of opinions I have dragged with me so far
through life, and instead take a genuinely fresh look at things.
Usually it's the speed of technological change that forces that
rethink. In a recent column I confessed to reconsidering the

nuclear power option. In response I was deluged with up-to-date information, mostly urging me to see the downside of nuclear power. I was accused of being a pawn of Blair's softening-up strategy.

Next on the agenda for a rethink was abortion. I am of the feminist generation and a supporter of a woman's right to choose. I am still, of course, rooted in those ideas. But the British Medical Association's debate about bringing the twenty-four-week limit down to twenty weeks seems to deserve attention. I have reported on abortion from many different angles. I have stood outside abortion clinics in America confronting anti-abortionists who seek to glue the locks, threaten the patients and even attack the medics. I have discussed sex classes with schoolchildren and debated whether Britain's high rate of teenage pregnancy was the result of too much sex education or too little. On the evidence: too little. I have many friends who have had abortions without the trauma and tragedy that the pro-lifers would have you believe would follow. But I am reassessing for several reasons.

First, what we know of the sentient nature of the maturing foetus is getting more detailed. I find that the photographs of foetuses supposedly 'walking in the womb' tell us nothing new, and their use by pro-lifers to win support for their cause is highly distasteful. But we do know more now than we did about the child in the womb. The scans, the tests, the monitoring of development during pregnancy all suggest that there is now broad agreement that in mid-pregnancy we are dealing with a foetus, moving in a very real way towards the status of a pre-birth baby.

Second, any woman who has sex without any protection against pregnancy has recourse to far more options than she once did. Among them are the morning-after pill, plenty of accessible family advice centres, enlightened GPs, school counselling, not to mention friends with phone numbers and useful addresses. The networking systems of women are broarder than they were in the days when student contemporaries of mine had recourse – without success – to drinking gin and jumping off tables. No woman, surely, should find herself at twenty-four weeks suddenly in need of an abortion she couldn't have had at twenty weeks.

I am up for a debate on the matter. I know that in the minds of lobbyists this will be interpreted as a weakening of my former position, the first concession to the enemy in a battle for hearts and minds. It is in fact no such thing. To radically readdress the issues that fired one's youth is not to give in to the religious right. It is merely to consider new information as it becomes available and to judge it with an open mind. Likewise, those who so doggedly resist assisted suicide and euthanasia may one day come to reconsider the dogmatic certainty of their views. At either end of life's span, the crucial line between being alive and not being alive is being scientifically and ideologically challenged. Bring it on, I say.

~

THERE WAS A DAY WHEN I thought the world would end. We all thought so, and not just in Britain. From 27 October 1962, Kennedy and Khrushchev played nuclear poker over the installation of nuclear weapons on the soil of Cuba. Kennedy said, 'Back off or else ...' It was the 'or else' that worried everyone. We spent some forty-eight hours in minute-by-minute expectation of a flash of light in the sky. Would the flash come first, and then a long lingering death, or would central London be taken out early in the Third World War? It's hard to convey to later generations what that felt like. And can that feeling ever be any more than anecdotage, the tiresome retelling and perhaps embellishing of episodes that have no relevance today? Can we ever learn from history? And if so, what is there that is useful to know?

With the issue of nuclear power back on the political agenda, my natural impulse is to clench my teeth and insist, as I always have, 'Not that way, not that way'. And yet times and circumstances change. After all, there was once a time when I cheered the news from Hiroshima. As a child I knew nothing of politics and strategy. I simply believed you had to have a bigger bomb than your enemy, hit them hard and win the war. That had been our single objective for six years and suddenly victory was ours. To my childish thinking this was unqualified good news. It was only later that I read of Robert Oppenheimer's judgement: 'I am become death, the destroyer of worlds.'

The mindset of the child is transformed into the mindset of the nuclear disarmer. The Campaign for Nuclear Disarmament wasn't born in an abstract world of busybodies with nothing else to do on Easter weekends than take the Aldermaston road. It was born of a very real and immediate threat. In the late 1950s both America and China were testing hydrogen bombs in the atmosphere. In 1957 there were forty-two such tests above ground. Soon strontium 90 was detected in milk. And I had a small baby.

Being anti the bomb easily segued into being against all nuclear power. Nearer home in 1957 there had been a major nuclear accident at Windscale, which released radioactive material into the atmosphere of Cumberland, up to ten times the normal level. Windscale later changed its name to Sellafield in the hope people would forget. But I was back there decades later, reporting for television on a cluster of leukaemia cases. No one played on the beach any more and there was talk of deformities among cattle. Nuclear power plays a long hand.

Alarm about nuclear power is real enough, but history sometimes doesn't go the way you expect. Some people in the late 1950s were so keen to escape imminent immolation they considered seeking refuge on remote islands. One such was Tristan da Cunha, the remotest island in the world. People began to make enquiries, even plans. Then in 1961 it suffered such a severe volcanic eruption that the entire population had to be evacuated to the UK. You can't always get it right.

The mindset has changed again. Today we are up against global warming and a dependence on fossil fuels that are not only running out but are to be found in places where they cause political mayhem. The role of oil in modern politics will be one of the regular exam questions for history undergraduates well into the twenty-first century. The odds at present are that global warming will wreak more havoc across the planet than nuclear-fuelled power stations, even with the unresolved problem of radioactive waste.

I was recently in Great Yarmouth and saw out at sea the great wind farms in action. They are sprouting up all over the place, predictably prompting objections from local people who don't want them to spoil their view. Besides, the protesters tell us, renewable energy is so costly and needs such extensive investment for small returns that we need to think again. In an Oxford debate in 2005 the discussion dealt with all the many aspects of renewables, from which the nuclear element alone was excluded. But the debate cannot be long delayed and in 2006 a decision is coming ever closer.

Changing your mind gets harder as you get older. You arrive at a world-view that seems the sum total of all life's lessons. So it is with me. It sits comfortably to be anti-nuclear power. I conjure up the evidence of my life: the nuclear race, strontium 90 in the milk, the Windscale disaster. But now I'm beginning to think it isn't enough. I'm going to have to think it all through again.

~

BEING ILL TEMPORARILY and confined to home has given me a different take on the world. I'm reading more and watching great swathes of television. And what do I find: it seems suddenly that a whole lot of people want to try their hand at being a teacher. It's too late for me, of course, but it did prompt a few of those 'what if ...' thoughts, the sort many of these would-be Mr Chips may be weighing in the balance.

Two wholly divergent pictures are coming across at the moment. First there is the beguiling television recruitment campaign from the Teacher Training Agency, showing cheerful and attractive pupils interacting amiably with smiling teachers who are finding this new challenge rewarding. Their own 'what if ...' is turning out well. On the TTA website I read of one such example: a lawyer hitting forty who used to work with criminals but now feels fulfilled and supported by those around him. Perhaps having been a lawyer helps him keep order in class.

The next witness for the positive side was ITV's wonderful play, broadcast in 2005, *Ahead of the Class*, starring Julie Walters as Marie Stubbs, the retired Scottish teacher who returned to tackle the distressing legacy of St George's comprehensive after the murder of its headmaster Philip Lawrence. This was real lump-in-the throat viewing. Our heroine talked of 'old-fashioned common sense', displaying the vintage values of discipline and love – ones my generation grew up with and still shares – which brought her success within fifteen months. A dream 'what if ...' for many of those still fresh with enthusiasm.

It all looks so easy in the ads and for Marie Stubbs. It isn't so for many of us. When I tried to be a supply teacher, back in the 1950s, I wanted to help make the world a better place, put something back into society, get a quality of life that spoke of human values. There were all the high ideals we see creeping back among those disenchanted with heartless and competitive career options. But it didn't work for me, a matter of temperament perhaps. I was hopeless at discipline and the children were running around the class, throwing things or hiding in cupboards. Pandemonium! Classroom disorder isn't new. That old-fashioned insistence on authority and obedience that I'd grown up with was by then already out of the window.

So where did things go seriously wrong? My own schoolday lessons had been formal and unquestioning. We sat in neat rows and took down 'the facts' in notebooks, which we conned by heart and regurgitated for exams. Talking in class was a detention offence, dipping the pigtails of the girl in front into the inkwell of your desk brought a swift visit to the headmistress. The slightest step out of line was instantly jumped on. We grew up orthodox and conformist, but secretly seething with rebellion. That rebellion was to come out later in our lives ... Witness the 1960s.

So whatever (former) Education Secretary Ruth Kelly was proposing, the heavy authoritarian route was not the way to go. I've learnt since, with children of my own, that they flourish best with love, friendship and genial control. That's what the ads try to show. In many cases children aren't getting these things even in their own homes. I can cite as evidence the television series *Little Angels*, a horrendous recital of small children running rampantly wild, manipulating their families into chaos and dysfunction. These children arrive at their primary school already disruptive, bullying wreckers. It's what they've grown up with.

Now comes the Ofsted report bearing out all I've been witnessing. Bad behaviour among a few is radically affecting the many, discouraging teachers, perhaps putting off those eager new recruits. Clearly no one wants this to happen. Even disruptive pupils can't be having much fun if they are being forced to go to schools where they aren't happy.

It's more than education; I think it's a multi-generational problem. Education was once seen as the guarantee of a job for life. That's no longer so. It was also seen as encouraging pleasure in learning for its own sake. That satisfaction seems to have migrated to the opposite end of the demographics. The Third Age movement, dedicated to lifelong learning for older people, is booming; there are some 550 groups around the country. There's no dipping of pigtails in the ink for them; they're all keen enthusiasts. Truly, education is often wasted on the young.

In the meantime, the Tomlinson recommendations (of October 2004) were given widespread support across the teaching profession. I was enthusiastic, keen to see how those vocational courses would give restless and disgruntled young people the responsibility of apprenticeships. They should engage them in sports enterprises, I thought, in youth theatres, music making, dance groups – make being alive a wonderful experience. Some of us haven't as much of it left as they have so it's no surprise that we value it more. I wonder whether that remarkable teacher we all sympathized with in the television play would agree.

~

I AM MADE THOUGHTFUL ABOUT what it is to be old by some of the letters I receive. Receiving letters – especially handwritten ones – is a particular pleasure of old age. Keeping in touch becomes increasingly important as the ranks of contemporaries thin out. Since writing my autobiography I have heard from a whole clutch of school friends, as well as signing copies for my son's former teacher and my sister's closest friend. The writing of my life story has prompted memories in others and they wrote to share them. So letters keep arriving. Kingsley Amis once told me that every morning when he heard that day's post thudding onto the mat, his first thought was always: 'There might be a letter from Philip.' Such was the closeness of his friendship with the poet Philip Larkin. Letters are a daily treat.

Sometimes they are more. Recently a correspondent wrote about another kind of life than mine. He has to struggle by on a modest pension, takes in lodgers to help out and is trying to hold on to his house for the sake of the children. It was a kindly letter, simply drawing attention to the many different shapes our later years take, remarking on my apparently busy social life but concluding: 'Every garden grows differently.'

None can have grown more differently than that of Audrey Hingston, who at the age of seventy-six became the sole carer of her husband Eric, whose health was deteriorating badly. They lived in a flat in Plympton, Devon, above the butcher's shop run by James, Mr Hingston's son from his former marriage. Audrey and Eric had married – a second time for both – in 1985 and were growing old together. His illness proved too much. It seems Audrey became distressed and then depressed about caring for Eric. She did the unthinkable. She took a kitchen knife and killed him while he was sleeping. She then compounded the crime by trying to cast the blame on others, inventing a story of a couple of burglars and going through with a police press conference appealing for help to find them. The whole charade fell apart and finally Audrey Hingston, who was eighty-one years old, was sentenced to two years in prison for what she had done. She was Britain's oldest woman prisoner.

What good did it do to have this woman in prison? On the news footage of her shown on television, she looked frail and bewildered, and I imagine she was not putting on a performance designed to deceive anyone. She was unlikely to be a threat to the public, as her crime was entirely within a personal and domestic context, and although her sentence was a relatively short one and she was released from prison at the end of 2004, serving just a year in custody, such a length of time when you are eighty-one constitutes a larger proportion of your remaining days than it would for someone younger. Both her defence counsel and the prosecution called for psychiatric reports, the gist of which was, I gather, that she was suffering from depression and not entirely responsible for her actions. Mrs Justice Hallett spoke at Plymouth Crown Court of both the wickedness of trying to blame others but also the extent of Mrs Hingston's solitary suffering. 'Unfortunately,' she declared, 'no one realized, when you sought help for your illness, the extent of it.' But, she went on, a prison sentence was necessary. 'I feel I have no alternative.'

Lawyers from both sides appeared to agree with this. There was no appeal against the sentence. Audrey Hingston was in Eastwood Park women's prison in Gloucester, where she was visited by her family and designated 'an enhanced prisoner', which meant that she had her own room, with shower, and the right to lock herself in at night. I am told she got on with other prisoners.

So far, so legally correct and, in prison terms, benign. But I am left with a picture of an eighty-one-year-old woman who cared for a sick man without the support she needed. I can't help feeling that ageing carers, the sole people responsible for looking after those they love, should have more formal support from society's network of welfare. It is a tragic aspect of what the old can expect.

~

IN THE SUMMER OF 2005 I found myself a target and I was not sure what to make of it all. I was right there in the beam of the searchlight alongside millions of others who had been waving from the shadows for years only to see the light of hope and comfort shining kindly elsewhere. Now suddenly we were all made visible; the sights of political big guns were trained on our interests. I was targeted on at least three separate counts. And with ten weeks still to go before I was expected to deliver up my vote, I supposed I was meant to feel meek gratitude for having been noticed at all.

First, I was targeted as a pensioner. The needs of those who are no longer earning was at last being taken seriously. There's no doubt that, at whatever scale you once earned, your income falls in retirement. That's a shock most people have to live through and accommodate. It isn't easy. Only those with the plushest investments and lavish company pensions will avoid having to make a lifestyle adjustment that can be painful, even traumatic. So along came the siren call of Michael Howard's proposal: he was offering me the direct bribe of a discount on my council tax bill that could be as much as £500. It would, he claimed, help 5 million pensioners who had been clobbered by the steep rises of recent years. So far, so good. But strangely there was one group that such a rebate wouldn't help at all, and they were the poorest pensioners of all. They, of course, already got a means-tested reduction and the Tories seemed to think that was enough. So while their election promise applied to me, in my middle-class comfort, it didn't reach the truly needy. How much bolder it would have been to raise the single pension to £105 and then pledge to keep it tied to prices. Meanwhile, pensions weren't even mentioned among the six rather vacuous New Labour promises that had until then led their campaign. One up to the Tories there.

Second, I was being targeted as a woman. An Age Concern survey showed that older voters – those over fifty-five – were twice as likely to vote as those under fifty-five. But two thirds of women over fifty-five would vote on election day, even though one in five of them was undecided at the time whom to vote for.

Older women are mindful of just what it meant to get the vote. The span of their lives puts them in closer touch with those early suffragette struggles. Their own mothers and aunts may have passed on their recollections of what went on: the meetings, the abuse, the imprisonments and the violence used against them. To be indifferent to electoral politics would be a betrayal of their cause. For younger women, the suffragettes are merely a subject on the syllabus. Poignant history, of course, but hardly a personal legacy handed down and to be acted upon.

So what would woo older women? Beyond pensions, we could be expected to care about the National Health Service. We grew up when it was the focus of the country's social contract, an institution that helped define the public good, available as a right and equal to all. We have seen it transformed by market forces, subject to public finance initiatives, subcontracted to profit-driven companies that can't even keep the hospital wards clean. We have long memories and may not think much of New Labour's so-called 'radical' reforms.

Third, I was being targeted because I was a floating voter. Women were significantly more undecided about whom to vote for than men. Just before the 2005 election, among women over sixty-five, 17 per cent had by then not yet made up their minds. I was one of them. I was not even sure I would vote at all and occasionally toyed with witty and contemptuous remarks to scribble across my postal vote. This was where I hit a conflict of personal impulses: my sense that it was my civic duty to vote – see the paragraphs above; my appreciation that the current government had done much good – the minimum wage, help for mothers and children, the New Deal for young people, devolution, a strong economy. Against those I set three huge

197

policy disasters: the refusal to implement the Tomlinson Report in what would have been landmark education legislation; the Iraq war with its continuing and multiplying ramifications; and the continuing assault on the rule of law in this country. That was my equation and I intended to continue floating until the last possible moment. The latest poll showed Labour only 3 per cent ahead so it was time for all the parties to get worried. We knew we could expect lots more promises and would decide, there and then, whether we believed them or not. Remember tuition fees? Who knows, I thought, I might well scribble that on my voting paper.

~

THE 2005 ELECTION held my attention to the end. One of the ideas up for consideration was Michael Howard's promise to cut inheritance tax. It was not something I wanted to hear. Indeed, I disliked the idea of appealing to the miserly instincts in human nature even unto the grave. I'd rather have seen inheritance tax increased. Of course, like many other things that happen to all of us – like dying and being forgotten – I'd rather it didn't happen to me. Again, like many people, I employ an accountant to get me the best deal possible within existing parameters. But when the time comes, I'll pay up willingly. Though, of course, I'll be dead at the time.

All fund-raisers know that one of the best tricks in the book is appealing to people to leave a bequest in their will. First, it gives a solemnity to the sticky business of handing over the moolah. It holds out the promise of one's name being spoken in grateful and respectful terms beyond the final trumpet. It suggests we could be remembered just a scintilla longer than might otherwise be the case. And if it's a big enough sum, it might get our name on a building, on a plaque for a bench, or on a nameplate inside a book. Something to keep the name lingering on. Most of all it won't be any kind of sacrifice. We won't feel the pain of parting from our money while we're still alive. It will in fact be donated by our heirs.

This business of inheritance sets up strange expectations. All our lives we manage our financial affairs as our temperaments and circumstances dictate. There are spendthrifts and misers in every income band. Mostly we in the middle zones manage, con-ventionally enough, to balance income against spend, so that overall, given a lurch into debt here and hopefully a windfall or two there, the equation comes out balanced with, all being well, enough to see us through to a modest lifestyle in retirement. That's the ideal. When things get better than that, and good fortune, hard work and our applied skills bring us the reward of riches, we start taking a longer view. We want the fruits of our labours to benefit those we love, individuals making their own way who were never part of our efforts, who haven't earned any of it but are in line simply by an accident of birth to wealth that is only theirs by virtue of the grim reaper. Nothing could be more patently unfair, more hostile to a natural justice we all profess to believe in: that each child born into the world is of intrinsic and equal value. Nothing perpetuates social inequality and dif-ferentials of opportunity more than that some young people grow up with their own trust funds, while others struggle from the start in the world of benefits, hand-me-downs and sink schools. Inheritance tax was created to tackle just such inequality.

Don't get me wrong. I'm not against wealth. I rejoice that pop stars and footballers who have natural talent, work hard to sustain it and give pleasure to millions should now be among our biggest earners, along with the writers of bestsellers and the makers of great films. This is a society that says it wants talent and effort rewarded. All I am saying is, 'So be it.' And let the children fend for themselves. I recall the Duchess of Devonshire explaining with much regret that on the death of the previous Duke, the state had taken a whopping great sum that had cut harshly into the fabulous Chatsworth estate. I mumbled my sympathies and asked by way of consolation how much they had left. Thirty-five thousand acres was the answer. I didn't feel too much regret, especially as the brilliant management skills of the present Duchess have since transformed Chatsworth into one of this country's most successful tourist businesses. She deserves her reward, however much it is.

For most of us lucky enough to have something to spare towards the end, there's always 'skiing' – spending the kids' inheritance. We have an understanding in my family that they get to share some of it now, rather than wait until I'm gone. Making funds available when a young family has a sudden pressing need feels good. And a modest bonanza – ten best seats for *Mary Poppins*, say – not only gave us all great and shared pleasure, it also defeated the tax man. While you're still alive it's yours to spend. After that it falls into the national tax pot. And everyone benefits.

How many families have sat around in the gloomy days after a funeral, waiting for the legacy that twenty years earlier could have transformed their lives? Alternatively, how many other families – brooding on the wayward habits of spoilt offspring – wish that inherited money hadn't melted away in a spendthrift life of international jet-setting? No, Michael Howard, I thought, we'll pay up in full when the time comes, in the interests of natural justice. But until then we're going to have a damned good time.

~

IT FEELS RATHER LIKE THE 1960S AGAIN. People are rising up in great numbers and making themselves heard. In 2005 they were rioting in France; Holland had its own version. Then came Bob Geldof inviting everyone to march on Edinburgh for the G8 summit. Those who couldn't get away from school were building up collections of charity armbands to indicate their solidarity with the needy, the sick, the poor. Taken individually each one of these events would seem a worthy enough gesture, but perhaps not much more than that. Taken together they amounted to more than the sum of their parts. It could be the first glimmer of change ... People are no longer passive about the way they are governed and the way the world is run.

In a tiny way I felt such stirrings in my own life. It concerned car parking fines, so my response was entirely self-serving. It did nothing to save the planet or relieve suffering. None the less I now learn that Londoners are up in arms about the ruthless and unforgiving ways of parking attendants. My own contribution goes like this. Lulled by the therapeutic effect of great art, I emerged from the John Soane Museum into the golden afternoon in Lincoln's Inn Fields. Turning along the empty pavement of the empty square, I saw a lorry with my little blue car aloft, driving off into the distance. I gave chase. They accelerated. The lights changed. I was almost abreast of the cab. The lights changed again and they moved off, but I was still in pursuit. At the next lights they pulled in. Perhaps they were imagining the headline: 'Senior citizen dies of heart attack in car rescue bid!' They were full of righteousness; it seems I had parked on a residents' parking space. This at 4 p.m. on a Saturday afternoon. I was, by the regulations, clearly guilty. My car was towed to Kentish Town pound and I had to follow and pay £200 to get it back.

My oversight was thoroughly understandable. There were simply no other cars there. There were spaces galore in which to park, acres of them, both residents' and ticket paying. I had breezed up, blessed my luck, parked at the nearest space and thought nothing of it. Surely instead of the inflexible application of top-down rules, people need to be free to exercise their own initiative? Anyone who has had cause to complain to a utilities company will understand.

This time it is Thames Water. I have a pipe that is leaking and am advised by my plumber to ask Thames Water to turn off the boundary stopcock in order that he can repair my own. Thames Water refuses. 'We don't do that,' they explain. 'It's not our responsibility.'

I am the very spirit of reasonableness: 'I am a customer of Thames Water, isn't that so?'

A reluctant 'Yeees ...'

'I have phoned you to ask for help.'

'Errr, well, yes.'

'Are you telling me you cannot give it?'

'That's right. We don't do that. You must ask your plumber.'

'But my plumber ...'

I won't go on.

I know we live too many rats to a cage, so that survival rather than collaboration is the way to get by. A resigned pragmatism now governs our choices. Schools? Move to within the catchment area of the best. Medicine? Use the NHS but go private to cut corners. Paying the mortgage? Take the job that makes an 'offer you can't refuse', rather than one you find fulfilling. There was a time, in the 1960s, when we tried to make choices that would bring benefits if everyone made the same ones. Thus it was that middle-class parents chose state schools and, by being active in parent/teacher bodies, helped raise the standards. But down the decades our loyalties have been privatized. How often have I been told by a supposedly left-wing friend opting for private education: 'Well, I had to put my child's interests first, didn't I?' The answer is, 'Not if you want the standards of your community to rise. In the long term their interests are best served by a society that feels itself to be fair and just.'

On a global level the balance may be tipping back towards a less selfish outlook. Who when confronted with the Darfur genocide dared to dismiss it with 'It's not my continent'? Whose response to poverty was 'Not my problem, pal'? Who is any longer happy to let the politicians get on with it? Some other spirit is stirring. Is it the revival of nationalist feelings? A new communitarianism? Or simply a more benign aspect of consumer capitalism? At the moment things are too much in flux for us to define it. But the flux itself is no bad thing. Welcome back the 1960s.

'You can judge your age by the amount of pain you feel when you come in contact with a new idea.'

PEARL S. BUCK

TEN

The Pace of Change

THIS IS A REFLECTION ON a world I know nothing about, the world of the future. Many of the latest developments that are around today – gadgetry and so on – seem to me like the culmination of the long march of progress, the newest and best that can be devised. Recently, however, I had the opportunity to interview the current President of the Royal Society and former Astronomer Royal, Martin Rees. He planted the notion that modern knowledge as it is today might well be in the merest foothills of innovation. He is a brilliant cosmologist who regularly deals in concepts of billions of years, so for him the idea of aeons of time stretching on without end comes easily enough.

In daily life we don't experience what goes on around us quite

THE VIEW FROM HERE

like that. As we approach our own end, it's natural to see the state of the world as somehow in its ultimate form, too. I once asked Lord Carrington, who had been Foreign Secretary in Mrs Thatcher's government and then Secretary General of NATO, what form of social organization he thought would follow capitalism. He looked blank for a moment, clearly puzzled, then offered his considered reply: 'I don't understand the question.' In 1992, Francis Fukuyama in his book *The End of History and the Last Man* had already argued that liberal democracy looked set to be, in socioeconomic terms, the peak of human achievement. No wonder then that when I grapple daily with small-scale but irritating gadgetry I tend, wrongly, to assume that these are the high days of technology. They might – terrifying thought – be only the beginning.

~

THE YOUNG ENJOY THEIR WIZARDRY. Each week, each day, new gadgets appear. Newspapers devote special pages to them. There's competition among consumers to own the latest. Once we become used to the technology of the new gadget there's scarcely a decent pause before there must be variations, different colours, shapes, sizes. Who would once have dreamt that some-one could become a millionaire simply by marketing different ring tones? A preoccupation with useless adjuncts to living is a self-defeating exercise. Soon the world's entire musical output will be on a gadget the size of a pea. And then we'll lose it.

Nothing dates like the latest technology. I am a great hoarder and have salted away over the years what amounts to a museum case of musical recordings. First up, and dating from my parents' days in the 1930s, an eight-inch 78 rpm recording, issued, it says on the label, by 'Broadcasting' and calling itself the Long Playing Record. In fact it is Nat Lewis's version of 'Little White Lies'. Next up in size, the eight-inch recording grew to ten inches — in my case Brunswick's records of Bing Crosby. Then came the twelve-inch — Regal's issue of Joe Loss's 'In the Mood', and Amelita Galli-Curci singing 'The Russian Nightingale Song'. Each of these, in its frail paper cover, stands lovingly preserved and unplayed on untouched shelves. I even have Beethoven's Ninth Symphony, all ten sides of it, on shellac. It was a nightmare to play, but at the time felt like the latest thing as, indeed, it was. Studio managers in BBC Radio in the 1950s, like myself, transmitted all classical music in this format, having to do clever things with two different turntables to make the piece run smoothly and avoid revealing the join.

What a treat it was when vinyl arrived. Surely this was the format of the future, so much lighter and flexible with it. There was no hissing sound and it wasn't a disaster if you sat on it by mistake. You could get not only the Beatles' albums *Sergeant Pepper* and *Abbey Road*, but the whole of Verdi's *Don Carlos* — with Tito Gobbi and Boris Christoff — on just eight sides of vinyl. How up to date could you be? We bought slowly and steadily, assessing the impact of each purchase on our limited budget. News that there was something newfangled on the way called a CD that would wipe vinyl off the map caused a certain alarm. Would we have to ditch the entire collection to keep up with change?

CDs have been my format of choice for a long time now but the vinyls are still there on the shelf with strange long-gone recordings, such as the Children's Corner version of *Alice in*

Wonderland and *Alice Through the Looking Glass*, narrated by Marjorie Westbury with Mary O'Farrell as the Red Queen. Who remembers such unusual recordings now? The accents are BBC 1950s but the narrative style is terrific and the grandchildren love them. So they remain, with their message that while the format may have changed the skills of the production team and the actors were as finely honed then as now, if not better.

I now have to face up to iPods. It's really a question of stamina. Learning new things at my age is not impossible, but it takes longer and needs more consistent concentration. I even doubt whether it will be worth it. I'm not convinced that this ubiquity of music is such a good thing. When I've spent time with music constantly in the background, I either cease to listen to it, which takes away the point, or I pay close attention and thereby lose concentration on what it is I'm supposed to be doing. Then again, is it really life-enhancing to have music always in your ears? I am sure statistics could show that cyclists wearing headphones are much more likely to have accidents. Besides, I prefer to have sound ringing out across a room, or at best across a concert hall, with all the attendant noises that indicate that this isn't simply an in-the-head experience but an occasion shared with others.

Most recently I discover the past can come to haunt you. Among the welter of New Year catalogues dropping on the mat came an offer for a retro turntable, designed specifically to play those old 78s, 33s and 45s. Some bright marketing spark has thought of wooing the grey pound. Not only does the sales pitch offer 'a nostalgic journey into yesteryear' but claims the casing is 'in classic retro-style'. I am suspicious, of course, and wonder just how authentic is all this 'retro' stuff? The first record player I was aware of was a completely unadorned black box, which opened onto a turntable clad in red velvet that was operated by a handle at the side. This must count as pre-retro, I imagine. This latest one looks like the fender of a 1950s American car. However, there is one thing to be said for it: you can't carry it around and you can't plug it into your ear. You simply have to sit at home – in the old-people's home, perhaps – put those old 78s on the turntable and relive your youth.

~

THEN AGAIN THERE'S THE TECHNOLOGY OF FILM. I deposited a reel of twenty-four exposures at the local chemist's to be developed, of our Bank Holiday outing to Lille. I was told they would be ready by the end of the day, which was fine by me: some six hours to wait, in mild anticipation, wondering whether that neat shot of the war memorial would have come out, or whether the faces would be in focus. I planned to organize the shiny prints in the subsequent days, date them and stack them away in old shoeboxes to join others on the shelves of events and people in my life. Once I might have had to wait several days to get them back, or if I'd posted off the film to one of those cut-price set-ups out of London, I'd be wondering whether I'd ever see them again at all. In the past, significant family records have gone totally astray in this way, with no redress. It was part of the hazard of the way things were.

I had also been browsing through a much older photographic collection taken by Roger Mayne in 1958 of that year's Aldermaston March. I was making an audio tape to accompany the Tate's

'Art and the 1960s' show, commenting on what the photograph revealed of the mood and events of the times. Even further back, I had visited an exhibition in Lille of photographs taken in China in the late nineteenth century by the French consul in what is now Chang Chou, across the straits from Taiwan, then called Formosa. Here was his record of individual Chinese – artisans and peasants, with their travelling kitchens and merchandise – meticulously posed, leaving a complete but formal record of what he had seen at first-hand.

The technology has changed and with it the nature of photography. It is not better or worse, merely different. People had been queuing up to teach me how to use a digital camera. They preach its merits: you get to see the picture to assess whether it's what you want. You feed what you have chosen straight into the computer, then send off copies or prints (I'm not sure whether these are even the appropriate words) to all and sundry so that they may have instantaneous access to shared holidays and family jaunts. Immediacy seems to be what it's about. Pictures, chosen on the spot, available instantly, distributed immediately. Am I wrong in thinking that without the anticipated waiting time, something could be lost? Would Roger Mayne have wiped his Aldermaston March because of a moment's impatience with its simple ordinariness? Would the French consul's eye for rather staged detail have survived the rush to capture the moment?

There is no doubt the ageing brain finds new things ever harder to do. Old domestic routines – how to cream butter and sugar to make a sponge cake, how to iron the cuffs and collars on starched shirts, how to shorten a hemline – remain clear and practical. But who does any of this any more? Who knows how to thread a sewing machine or patch a loose cover? And who cares? Today's answer is to throw out anything that develops a fault and buy the latest, most up-to-date model.

I have developed one or two tricks to help me remember any new instructions others give me. First, I only learn a very little at a time. 'Stop right there,' I insist when they have scarcely begun, 'that's enough to be going on with.' Then I scuttle away and say it over and over to myself, often using their own words out loud. Second, I write things down. There are yellow Post-its scattered throughout the house, reminding me of such matters as details of batteries or ingredients, the name of an odd but promising website. Third, I repeat a new skill and keep on repeating it until it becomes second nature. Thus I spent days copying things I didn't want onto floppies that I wouldn't keep, trying to get the routine to stick. Within the year floppy disks were a thing of the past and I then had to master the rewritable CD.

Eventually, of course, I bought a digital camera, which was just as well because within months Dixons announced they were withdrawing domestic sales of cameras that use good old-fashioned film because they believed that the world was already digital. Assumptions like this leave stranded many of us who began with a Brownie box camera. Once more I convince myself that I am finally up to date when, the next thing I know, my new mobile phone offers me a facility I hadn't anticipated: it will also take pictures and moving pictures at that. Soon I am swanning round the Rachel Whiteread exhibition in the Turbine Hall of Tate Modern, capturing the great white cliffs of her display in miniature and blurred pictures.

I am not sure why I am doing it, what purpose is served, or where the record will be stored, if, that is, I keep it at all. I finally decide that I am using this genuinely impressive technology simply because that's what it is. It is its own justification, serving no particular need, answering no pressing consumer demand, except the prevailing wish to be up with the latest gadget simply for its own sake, and to boast of it to friends and family. The satisfaction lasts but a brief moment because soon they have the same gadget too and the only thing that is of interest is 'what's new'.

Back home, however, there is nothing to take to the local developers, no roll of film to drop into those highly coloured freebie bags to send off to places in Devon whence they return a batch of shiny snaps within days. I have to do it for myself: transfer the pictures from the digital camera to the laptop, then view and judge, delete the pictures I judge inferior, until I have the hard core of what I want to keep. So far, so time-consuming. Then there are more choices. I can transfer them all to a disk, and/or I can make prints of those I would like to have. The prospect of having shiny prints to hand once again sends me off to the nearest shop where I plug the disk into a machine that prints out my choices. Otherwise I convert them through my printer onto sheets of special shiny paper on which they come out in varying approximations to the actual colours, making me long for the place in Devon that takes and processes old-fashioned film. Probably they've gone out of business.

Eventually my camera is overloaded with pictures and I need to delete most of them. This feels like throwing away negatives, ditching the equivalent of those caches of sticky black oblongs that still lurk in shoeboxes in attic cupboards. 'Delete?' the machine asks and I dither. Once gone, they will be lost to history. No one will unearth them decades hence and marvel at how we once lived. Yes, delete, I click. Life, after all, is fleeting and so too are photographs.

Only with the floppy disks consigned to the bin and the delete procedure completed do I lift my eyes from the laptop and there on my desk is the 1940s photograph of my schoolteachers seated in two neat rows, a sepia picture surviving from long ago, in a format that remained unchanged for decades. There they sit, the women who shaped and instructed me, ordered my moral welfare and supervised my manners. I once lived in awe of their power and their great age. Now I realize with a certain fond melancholy that I am much older than any of them were when they posed so long ago. Funny thing, photography. Funny thing, time.

~

THE BUSINESS OF KEEPING RECORDS is tricky if you've been in my line of business for thirty years or so. When the recording of television programmes first began, back in the early 1980s, my vanity was such that I quickly acquired a hugely cumbersome recorder so I could set up what I grandly called 'my archive'. This was my reaction to events in the 1960s when scarcely any of the live nightly programmes that I made for the BBC were recorded at all, and most of those that were had been wiped so that the BBC could use the tape a second time. Rare survivors include long interviews with Marcel Duchamp, Jacob Bronowski, Georges Simenon and Sir Kenneth Clark. Now, with this wonderful new video recording all would be different. The archive would swell, made up of interviews with David Hockney, David Sylvester, Alec Guinness and such.

It didn't work out like that. Technology roared ahead and in no time one-inch tape was obsolete and new finer techniques were in. The big VCR gave way to a smaller one. The new boxes of tapes were a different shape: the earlier boxes wouldn't play on the new machines. In the 1990s video recording reigned supreme. Nothing, surely, could improve on it. My shelves groaned with their neat black boxes. But since then we've got into DVDs and slim little sleeves of silver now keep the records. Don't think that's the end. Soon all our lives will be encoded in a microdot, just as in those old spy stories.

Who will ever sort them, watch them, store them? Will it be our descendants, or museums of bric-a-brac and ephemera? Perhaps our legacy will find its way to the car boot sales of the future, shuffling their stuff for the latest version of *The Antiques Road Show*, the programme where people care more about monetary values than intrinsic worth. I almost prefer the prospect – after my death – of the skips outside the door rattling to the sound of a lifetime's journey being ditched. Meanwhile I've just acquired a web-cam so I can send a neat little video with my e-mails around the world. It can only compound the problem.

~

ONE OF THE MOST STARTLING changes in technology, which intrudes into everyday life, is how often and continuously people are in touch. No one leaves the front door in the morning on the way to work without expecting to have contact with family and friends at several points throughout the day. Having a mobile phone clamped to your ear is the default mode of walking along the street. On the web, too, people log on to chat rooms across the world, making contact with total strangers. I sometimes wonder what it is they all have to say.

My own chat room experiences are strictly functional. Chat rooms have a kind of notoriety among the uninitiated. Isn't this where shadowy men groom naive young girls for elopement and seduction? Isn't this where people with odd tastes congregate to share their perversions? My first chat room experience was much along those lines. It took place in a porn factory in Amsterdam selling sex around the world. Callers made requests by e-mail of nubile young girls who then acted out these fantasies in the isolation of the factory's little studio. 'So much better,' one of them told me, 'than working the wet streets of Glasgow. Here there's no risk of broken glass in your face, no exchange of bodily fluids.' A modest enough improvement, but significant none the less.

I was making a television film about censorship at the time and in the way of involving the presenter in the action, was interviewing – fully clad, by the way – the young women about their work. Unsuspecting, I drifted within sight of the cameras. The response was instant from the chat room audience. From as far away as Indonesia came the queries: 'What's that old lady doing there?' You will understand why I didn't find it congenial.

This week's chat room was as different from that as possible and it took me back to a time in the 1970s when the late Dr Chris Evans – scientist, writer, inspiration – took me along to his workplace somewhere in West London and pointed at a small matchbox-like object mounted within a display case in the foyer. 'That,' he said, 'is a chip. It's about to change everything.' He then sat me down at a computer and got me to type my medical details onto the screen and then add a question concerning my health.

Miraculously, in a few seconds up came a reply. 'And that,' he declared triumphantly, 'came from California. Just imagine how this is going to transform medicine.'

And so it has. That's how this week I was able to get together with Professor Mike Richards, the National Cancer Director, at the offices of Breast Cancer Care in London and join with him in fielding questions coming up on the screen from women all around the country who had particular issues they wanted to raise. I learnt a lot that day, first about the illness. There is already so much knowledge out there; talk of taxanes and letrozole, of HER2 and sentinel node biopsy flowed freely. Women want to know and insist on finding out the latest information. Breast Cancer Care is dedicated to answering their questions. Once doctors were the high priests of medicine: the faithful flock didn't question their dogma. Now lay people – especially patients – are much more directly involved. Here were Shirley and Juliet, and Pat, coming together from different parts of the country to put their questions and discuss among themselves something of critical and intimate importance to them all.

Naturally I kept an ear alert for information that applied specifically to my age group. I had once believed that beyond a certain high-risk age group, you had somehow ridden out the storm and your chances of contracting breast cancer diminished thereafter. To my alarm I discover that I'm not the only one making this mistake and many people are unaware that the chances go on rising after the age of seventy. Well, they know now!

I was impressed by how quickly personal familiarity becomes the norm in the chat rooms. I can see how gullible teenagers could mistake this virtual contact for the real thing. I was also touched by the women's concern for each other and their easiness in talking personally. As the taxi driver drove me away he added his comment: 'You women are so good at getting together and helping each other. But who's worrying about my prostate cancer, that's what I want to know?' And what about other groups, I wondered? I did a little digging and found not only Friends Reunited but a clutch of other websites targeted specifically at older people. Although I portray myself as thoroughly clumsy when it comes to the internet, that doesn't mean I give up trying. I am in fact a champion of the internet for the old.

~

MEANWHILE THERE'S ANOTHER old-fashioned way of doing things that's on the way out. I shall miss the stub of pencil on a string and the makeshift wooden cubicles. I shall miss having a chat on the steps of the school with the canvassers from different parties, sharing an uneasy truce while they tick off who's been to vote. I used to do that myself in the 1950s, first as a student at Cambridge, then for the Hampstead Labour Party. In those days the Tories always got in. But it was being part of the whole circus that mattered, the political gossip, the speculation and even, gosh, the chance of meeting the candidates. I'm a postal voter now and it doesn't have the same buzz. There's no sense of occasion about marking a paper in my own kitchen. There's no great scope for political dialogue in asking a neighbour to witness my identity. But I shall certainly be voting, oh yes. It's just that I haven't decided who for yet.

Older people are the most likely to use their vote. We probably got involved decades ago when the parties had strongly differentiated ideals and you voted for the one that most matched your own. Now the parties round up a plausible medley of utopian wishes and dreams, adopt policies to match and hope to get themselves voted in. That's not the philosophy of principled governance, it's a strategic move by career politicians looking for personal promotion. Still, old habits of thought die hard. Growing old, by and large, means being suspicious of change.

Perhaps that's why only 30 per cent of retired people have internet access while 98 per cent of those aged between fourteen and twenty-two use computers. A recent survey by the Oxford Internet Institute showed that only 30 per cent of those over sixty-five bother with the new technology. For those over seventy-five, the proportion falls to 20 per cent. Perhaps, having settled for life as they know it, they simply don't want their lives transformed, and besides, taking to the internet requires certain acts of courage. First, you have to admit to yourself that you know less, quite substantially less, than your children and grandchildren. Old age was once supposedly a hallowed time of wisdom and experience. The whole concept has been turned on its head and we have to go seeking help from youngsters who are only now learning to ride a bicycle or swim a length. Unless we have children of universal charm and sympathy, we can find ourselves fobbed off, just when we are near to tears with exasperation. Still, they'll not want for Christmas presents to give you; I got *Basic Computer Skills Made Easy* the last time around.

Once you've faced down the family psychodrama of all this, there's the nature of the beast itself. The machinery goes wrong; the technology doesn't work; the systems break down and wipe out your efforts. I used to assume it was all my fault. I was old, I didn't

'Let others hail the rising sun:
I bow to that whose course is run.'

DAVID GARRICK

ELEVEN

Things Begin to Go Wrong

THIS IS THE LAST CHAPTER IN THE BOOK, so it deals with last things. Everyone moves towards their death at an unchanging pace. Yet even though some of us are ahead in the journey it is unusual for us to have any real sense of the moment's approach, unless, that is, we are knowingly terminally ill. I have a friend now in her ninety-seventh year, lively in spirit and wits, who was recently in hospital due to the effects of shingles that had lingered too long. How easy it would have been to assume her course was run. But that's not what happened. She, her family, and I too as someone who had known her over sixty years, believed there was more life for her to live. She came out of hospital in time for Christmas, wrote her usual Christmas cards in a clear and traditional hand and celebrated at the heart of her large family. It was not time for her to go, and no one thought it was.

But the thought recurs more often than it once did that the years if not the days are running out. For many of us, there is still lots to do, places to visit, younger families to watch grow, so the poignancy of those shadowy thoughts is all the more telling. Here is a diversity of my own reactions to what cannot, in the end, be avoided.

~

I FELL OFF MY BICYCLE while cycling around the walls of Lucca in Tuscany, not a wise thing to do at any age. Not a good idea at all in your seventies. Lucca is uniquely blessed in the whole of Tuscany in having a complete encircling wall with many of the gates and bulwarks of the original still in place. They haven't been used for defence since they were completed in the seventeenth century. Instead their broad summit has been lined with plane, poplar and elm trees, the whole circuit providing a delightful avenue for both locals and tourists to idle away the sunny hours. Here are large ladies exercising small dogs, dreamy lovers leaning in towards each other, fat sweaty men gesticulating their opinions and small flocks of families enjoying an outing on hired bicycles. We were of the latter company.

I should have known better. At my age you need to be in training for such exploits. It was over a year since I had cycled at all and that was at the Aldeburgh festival when I travelled along the sea front with around thirty others, emitting a medley of sounds that converged into some transient piece of contemporary music. The pace was slow, the ground level. No one remembers the music. At Lucca things were different. Forgetting my age – something I do all the time – I ploughed boldly up the slope ahead of the grandchildren only to come bouncing off and landed with a thud on my shoulder. Twenty-four hours and a large bag of frozen peas later, I was still in severe pain.

The old, more than most, need to be equipped with the paperwork of holiday insurance and health care, but the old, being forgetful, are most likely to neglect it. I was vaguely aware I had universal and comprehensive travel insurance but had left the details back at home. I had remembered to bring my E111 with me but hadn't got it stamped at the post office before I left. This was hopeless. My family were kind enough not to comment on my incompetence. Instead they took me to Lucca Hospital.

Things got better at once. Lucca is a small town and has one hospital, so no choice there. But who would want it when what was on offer was so good? The accident and emergency admissions were colour coded. Mine was blue/white, as least urgent. But instead of putting me at the end of one long queue, this coding referred me briskly and efficiently to the low-priority area. Here I was admitted within ten minutes, saw a doctor within a further ten, had an X-ray within the hour and then was back to see the same doctor. He looked long and hard at the X-rays and struggled to explain them in broken English, even as I was struggling with my fractured Italian. No bones were damaged. He used the word 'specialist', which is the same in both languages. My heart sank. It might mean a long wait, perhaps, appointments, they might tell me to come back tomorrow. Nothing of the kind. The specialist was two doors along and saw me within five minutes. I emerged with my arm in a sling and a prescription for hefty painkillers. I consulted my Berlitz phrasebook: 'Whom do I pay, where, how much?' No, no, nothing. Nothing at all. How could this be? I could only guess that there is an agreement within the European Union simply to offer the old of each country free treatment at all times. I didn't stay to find out. I left in high spirits at receiving such benign and swift medical care. The date of birth in my passport was all it had taken. At that moment, being old was almost worth it.

But will it be the same in other countries? According to Saga, more and more of the over-fifties – the target market for their holidays, insurance, etc – are travelling further afield. Currently Libya, Thailand and South Africa are among their list of destinations. They will take you scuba-diving in Borneo, ranching in Arizona and on a photographic cruise to Antarctica. Younger people express surprise as such exploits but they make total sense to me. Older generations have the time on their hands, the children have grown and gone, early retirement has taken worry and responsibility with it. Moving to a smaller home can provide a bit of cash to spare, and there's no time to lose. Leave it a year or two and you might not be so fit or so energetic.

But my recent experience has made me wary. We can't pretend to be younger than our age. We might feel frisky and full of beans, but the body has slowed, reflexes aren't what they were and bones are more brittle. We need to match our ambitions with our abilities, take along the insurance paperwork and not fall off the bicycle.

~

SOME TIME AGO I found myself spending time with smokers. It just so happened that life's events brought me into the company of old friends, smokers, as I had been, from their early years. I hadn't realized until then just how difficult their lives had become.

We had travelled from London on the same train and, once away from the railway's total ban, they stopped to light up. They did this, not on the platform or within the booking hall, because, who knows, it might have been in breach of some regulation or other. Instead they waited until they were well outside the station on the public pavement where, as yet, in the open air people are free to smoke. My friends are people of impeccable good manners, so later on they wouldn't dream of smoking in the car that had come to collect us for the Buxton festival. Again they waited. I began to grasp how much had changed and what was once common behaviour had become a hounded and persecuted habit, engaged in furtively by people who are made to feel outcasts.

By now alert to their problems, the first thing I noticed on entering the terrace of the hotel was a 'no smoking' notice on each of the dinky tables where residents might be expected to take tea or an evening drink. Except that we wouldn't. Instead my friends made for their room, a smoking room reserved in good time where, alone and isolated from the rest of us, they could give in to their wicked addiction.

It was a fine summer evening, and the marquee outside Buxton Opera House provided both a bar and open air where smokers could indulge. Even so, I sensed my friends' self-consciousness at doing something other people might find offensive. They hovered at the edge of the crowd. So it was that later, after dining in a private room at another hotel, they removed themselves to an open window where again the curling smoke rising from their cigarettes might not incur the community's wrath. I began to wonder whether we weren't getting things out of proportion. They were not breaking the law; they were lifelong smokers who had either failed to give up or had chosen not to do so and their lives were constrained from minute to minute by the rules imposed upon them.

Next day I was reminded of my own place in this story. I was signing copies of my autobiography when I looked up and after only a moment's pause recognized a teacher of mine from long ago days at Stockport High School. We fell into reminiscences and almost her first remark was: 'I remember when you started smoking; you must have been about seventeen!' She had been the escorting teacher on a sixth formers' trip by coach to Holland, and away from home for the first time many of us took to wicked ways. I was to smoke from then on, settling at around forty a day, through two pregnancies, and only giving up at the age of forty. My children grew up in smoke-filled rooms. Throughout the 1960s I regularly smoked while conducting interviews on television. Smoking was an accepted part of the culture. Even now, faced with one of life's brutal events – a divorce, say, or a bereavement – I resort briefly to the old, familiar comforter. It always feels good.

Yet I have strong personal reasons to be anti-smoking. My younger sister and only sibling, who smoked heavily all her life, died of cancer seven years ago in her late fifties. It was her breast rather than her lungs where the cancer struck, but I have long thought that heavy smoking contributed to her general unfitness. Yet even here my sympathies are divided. As she lay in hospital, struggling in her final months, one of the few solaces she had left was the pleasure she took in having a cigarette. The rules were severe. Once or twice she staggered to the toilet for a secret puff, only to have the nurses banging unceremoniously on the door. On occasion, I escorted her stooped figure, moving slowly down the ward, to the open-air fire escape at the far end, where she and other frail figures were allowed to take their modest comfort. Nicotine is addictive; smokers need it badly. People of my generation who smoked without qualms in their earlier years may find it hard to give up. Some of them do. Others don't want to. And sometimes they break the rules.

This happened at a summer's Royal Academy dinner a year or two back. The Royal Academy is a 'no smoking' building. None the less, after the loyal toast, at that moment in the proceedings when the host used to declare, 'You may now smoke,' many were the sideways looks to see who might disobey. Eventually I believe it was David Hockney who broke rank, together with Maggi Hambling, and it wasn't long before the giveaway wisps of smoke were curling upwards from the glittering tables. People can take only so much regimentation of their personal lives. When they feel the might of the majority oppressing their personal preferences they will revolt. We have not yet become a Prohibition state, but it's wise to recall that when America banned alcohol, speakeasies, smuggling and a hoodlum mafia culture prospered.

I am glad that smoking is banned in our public buildings. I choose a non-smoking area in restaurants and bars. I am troubled if there is too much smoke around where I am eating or drinking. I am thankful the packets carry heavy warnings. But haven't we become a little frantic over the whole matter? The law banning smoking in any enclosed public buildings will come into force in 2007. I attended the debate in the House of Commons where I heard speaker after speaker declare their support and denounce in passionate terms the danger passive smoking offered to barmaids. There was even talk of banning it in prisons, where it must be one of the prisoners' remaining consolations. I feel uneasy at this unrelenting pursuit of those who want to smoke. Smoking is a freely made choice, like drinking alcohol, and although you can be addicted to both, there must remain aspects of behaviour on which the nanny state doesn't dictate. Yet the same government that plans to get heavier and heavier with smokers has at the same time extended the licensing laws for drinkers. Odd, that.

~

THE PHONE RINGS. Bad news: another friend has breast cancer. Surely not another one. I'm beginning to feel anxious that in answering the phone call I don't sound surprised or shocked enough. In truth I want to groan and say, 'Oh, not you too', consigning them, by the implied multitude of others, to the status of a rather tiresome, complaining rabble. But that's not what people want to hear nor is it how they want to be treated. They want their own condition to be unique, the cause of specific panic, which, of course, it is for them. Despite all the improvements in drugs and treatment, breast cancer remains genuinely life-threatening, so the phone call must be taken very seriously indeed.

How odd that in the generations that follow us, young women are eager to have their breasts sliced open and lumps of breast-enhancing synthetics pumped into them. How late in life does such an operation become viable? And what happens when breast enhancement meets up with breast cancer? Might there be a time somewhere in early middle age when there's a collision of interests, the synthetic and the malign vying for dominance? It doesn't bear thinking about.

What is clear is that breasts matter more to us than, say, bunions or warts, or even hip joints and rheumatism. The other conditions may be painful but they don't strike at the core of women in quite the same way. St Agatha had hers cut off by the Romans and went straight to heaven, only to appear in many a gruesome painting – Flemish school, usually – carrying the severed pair in a little dish.

If these surreal fantasies seem inappropriate to human suffering that is happening right now, ascribe them to a certain hysteria on my part. As popular psychology will tell you, hysteria can conceal true feeling. That's because my younger sister died of breast cancer, a close friend had an operation for the same condition last week, another is only a little further along the treatment conveyor belt, and many who were diagnosed with it are walking tall and proud, having put the trauma behind them. Breast cancer is part of my extended family.

For years as they get older women have been on a rollercoaster ride of hopes and fears. First the good news: new drug trials, less brutal surgery. Bad news: HRT increases risk, there's talk of it being a Western lifestyle disease. Good news again: an entirely new drug could make all the difference. Bad news again: HRT doesn't help keep the heart healthy as was once thought, though it's still beneficial in avoiding osteoporosis. (This is a side issue, I know, but if you read the medical pages you get caught up in the cross-currents and an outbreak of hypochondria.)

My friend's own personal rollercoaster indicates just how up-front both medicine and women are about these things now. On a Wednesday she went into hospital for the appropriate operation. The whole thing was over and she was back home by the same evening. The following Monday she was a lively presence at my book publishing jamboree. A visit to the specialist on Thursday and on Friday of that same week the stitches came out. The very next day she flew to Cape Town on BBC business. This seems to me stoicism of a high order, probably more than the BBC deserved or were even aware of. She returned at the end of the month to face six months' radiation.

Meanwhile there's news of a battle lost. The redoubtable Clare Venables, one of the outstanding spirits of British theatre in the last two decades, lost to her cancer. I hadn't known she was ill and had one of those heart-stopping moments on opening the obituary pages. It's the one headline no theatre person wants to have.

Women around me are having to deal with breast cancer on a daily basis – the unwelcome news, the friend's op, the sudden obituary. Are men, I wonder, aware of the scale of what seems to me like an epidemic? Tony Blair can, quite rightly, alert the medical resources of the country to come to his aid in an emergency. I only hope he reminds Cherie to find time, between important legal cases and caring for her family, to go for a mammogram. She may be a patron of Breast Cancer Care but women have a habit of making a fuss about the care of others and forgetting to care for themselves.

~

'WHERE DID I LEAVE THE CAR KEYS?'

'I came upstairs to fetch something, but what was it exactly?'

'I'm aware that I know this person but her name has gone completely out of my head.'

All of these dilemmas will be familiar enough to anyone over fifty. Although the memory declines with age it does not do so entirely of course. The paradox is that at the very time when vivid images of an event that happened in childhood come abruptly and unexpectedly to mind, we aren't able to recall the address of a friend we visited yesterday. On the one hand we can wallow in nostalgia for Proust-like walks below the hawthorn blossom, but the next moment have to apologize for some stupid lapse: the blank left by a familiar name or fact that makes us feel both embarrassed and foolish.

When exactly should we worry? One of the early symptoms of Alzheimer's disease is forgetfulness, and a survey published in 2004 at a conference on dementia in Rome found that the British are the slowest to report their symptoms, which leads to the longest interval between noticing the first symptoms and a diagnosis of Alzheimer's. From first symptoms to diagnosis takes about ten months in Germany. In Britain it takes thirty-two months. That's far too long. The sooner symptoms are reported, the sooner available drug treatments can be used. If diagnosis comes late, the drugs aren't effective. Dr David Wilkinson, a consultant in Old Age Psychiatry from Southampton, puts this down to British stoicism, which he sees as a public health problem where Alzheimer's is concerned. Older people battle on without telling anyone, believing their symptoms are part of normal ageing, while their close family are both fearful and awkward about suggesting tests. Dr Wilkinson also believes an unspoken culture of ageism keeps funding low in this area of medicine.

But what is part of normal ageing, and what is a treatable disease? I am almost neurotically alert to such changes. Some years ago I sped off to the doctor complaining of a bad memory and was despatched by him for some fancy tests. Among other things, I was given numbers, very long numbers, to recite backwards; next I was shown a vast spread of photographs of different physiognomies and then given a complex quiz about them. At the end of these and many more such tests, my results were analysed and I was told I had nothing to worry about. That didn't stop me, of course. Apparently, again according to Dr Wilkinson, there's something he calls 'memory neurosis' among perfectly healthy fifty- and even forty-year-olds, who are simply worried about their declining powers. What I want to know is how can you tell one condition from the other?

I also recently went to have my hearing tested. There's no doubt that for older people the background noise of a crowded room in full cry makes hearing the person next to you very hard indeed. It's a genuine social handicap. Yet the option of giving up on party-going is not to be contemplated. So I was put through another set of tests and was shown the resulting chart of my hearing. There it was, a line representing the capacity of each ear that slid down the page where a young and buoyant ear would have held steady. 'Oh my God, I'm going deaf!' No, no, I was reassured, I was merely experiencing the decline considered to be customary for my age. It seems a fine distinction and one to keep an eye – or ear

– on. I continue to monitor my performance in loud and crowded places.

We have to be brave about this. It is something we need to confront before it gets too bad. A couple of years ago I had a minor part in the film *Iris*, in which Judi Dench played the part of the novelist Iris Murdoch as she declined into Alzheimer's. My role was that of the television interviewer asking a question at just the moment when Iris has her first confused lapse of memory. It was a brief and poignant moment that presaged all that was to come. The film's director, Richard Eyre, had a parent who suffered from Alzheimer's and I believe he felt that making the film would familiarize us all with its symptoms as well as enlist our sympathy for its sufferers. From the conference in Rome comes further news that this is essential.

British stoicism may be one explanation for why we take so long to seek a diagnosis. The other is that Alzheimer's carries a stigma; people are ashamed of being sufferers. They would rather tell themselves, 'Oh, it's just getting old', as a comforting response to their fears about having the disease we all dread. But Alzheimer's is a specific condition. The medics are working on it. There are drugs to help. We shouldn't hold back. Society may want to dodge the issue, but we can't afford to. And while we're about it, we could subscribe to Alzheimer charities too! If the old don't, who will?

~

THE LAB AT SCHOOL WAS always a mysterious place, most particularly the shelf that contained the specimens. They were distributed in jars lined up inside a cupboard whose glass doors were never opened. There was a strong smell of formaldehyde. One jar regularly caught my eye: it was of a small human foetus, its large head curving round, suspended in some yellow liquid. It was an object of awe and dread, a dead thing swaying gently in its opaque, watery space. It never occurred to me that it had other resonances: a grieving mother, a disappointed family. It was simply a specimen. Once you were dead and in a lab, that's what you were.

Not any more. Ever since the disclosure about Alder Hey Children's Hospital, when it came to light that organs of children had been stored for research without adequate consent, body parts have been the subject of tender concern. It seems that when people signed a consent form that told them that the consequences might involve 'the retention of tissue for laboratory study' or even 'for the treatment of other patients for medical education and research', they didn't take in that it might mean their loved ones ending up as a specimen on a laboratory shelf.

Would that be such a terrible destiny? After all, the other options aren't particularly attractive. 'Ashes to ashes, dust to dust' certainly carries the poetic notion that we are returning to the earth from which we sprang. But England's leafy country churchyards are crowded these days. You have to have family connections or pull strings to get in. Otherwise there's cremation and the scattering of ashes around a rose tree, perhaps, or into a favourite river. I know someone – the relation of a victim of the Munich air disaster that killed Matt Busby's Manchester footballers – whose ashes are scattered on Manchester United's ground. Apparently, it's considered a great favour. There are many requests and only a few are chosen. The idea of death at sea has its appeal, made lyrical by Shakespeare's imagination: 'of his bones are coral made...' But you would need to die either over-indulging on a luxury cruise or being flung from a yacht in a high gale and I don't fancy either.

This leaves the option of doing something useful with what remains of you. I know people walking around today with bits of other people fully functioning inside them. One has someone else's heart, the other a liver. Both organ donations came in the nick of time to restore my pale and waning friends to the vigorous and creative people they had been before their illness struck. One even believes he acquired, along with his new liver, a deeper and more thrilling taste in music. Both live with a sense of daily gratitude for what has happened. That can't be such a bad destiny for bits of what was formerly you. There may be even more exotic destinations. J. G. Ballard writes in his autobiographical *The Kindness of Women* of the tender, even loving relationship that he struck up as a young medical student with the female cadaver he was dissecting. (Make allowances: the man's a genius!)

So what arrangements have I made? Clearly it's important to sort matters out while your step is still sprightly, because for close relations bereavement is no condition in which to make heart-wrenching decisions. Have I decided? No. I am stopped in my tracks by an appalling thought. My body and its available spare parts are probably too old and run-down to be of much use. My liver has been given a rough time by a lifetime's pleasure in wine; a taste for sirloin steaks and cream teas has probably furred up my arteries. I smoked until I was forty, so my lungs will be no good to anyone. Besides, I read that heart, liver and lungs are only likely to be useful until the age of sixty-five.

That leaves kidneys – the age limit there is seventy-five. I used to carry a kidney donor card, but it seems to have gone missing. There was a proposal to make donation automatic, so that you only needed to make arrangements if you wanted to opt out and take your kidneys with you. That idea has been rejected, it seems. So I'll need to forage for that old card again. The best news is that there is no age limit for the donation of corneas from the eyes. So perhaps one day far hence, I shall still be gazing fondly across that candlelit table, at someone else's Valentine. Gruesome? Well, it's better than being in a jar on the laboratory shelf.

~

DYLAN THOMAS GAVE US BAD ADVICE. As a young man he penned one of his best and most anthologized poems. A devoted son, he wrote with a son's devotion. Passionate with grief, he urged his father: 'Do not go gentle into that good night. Rage, rage against the dying of the light.' The father died notwithstanding. And the poet son followed him only a year later, his own rage of self-destruction cutting him down at thirty-eight years of age, far sooner than his benign old father. Ever since then 'Do not go gentle' has become the anthem for approaching death, taken up by generations as the proper way to engage the grim reaper. With so many of us no longer believing in life after death, desperate that those we love should survive as long as possible, it seems a plausible sentiment to prolong life at any cost. It values the faintest surviving breath above the silent, barren beyond. And medical practice goes along with that to a considerable degree.

It wasn't always so. Another poet in another age took an altogether more sublime, if to us totally baffling view of life's end. John Donne, the seventeenth-century metaphysical poet, celebrated his highly charged erotic youth, defying the etiquette of James I's court by eloping with the love of his life, but later on developed a deeply devout maturity, as Dean of St Paul's, where his brilliant sermons drew the crowds of the day. He left behind a letter in which he wished that illness was not involved at the end of his life, because he feared it might spoil the enjoyment that he might otherwise take in his dying, an experience he understood to be on the very brink of being brought into the presence of God. 'Think then, My soule, that death is but a Groome,/Which brings a taper to the outward roome.' He even went to the trouble of posing in his shroud while they made his effigy, the one monument in old St Paul's to survive the great fire of London. It stands even now in the place he designated when he presided there. It strikes today's visitors as rather eerie, if not grisly.

Since Donne's time the matter of our final days has become inextricably bound up with the law. Any type of euthanasia – incidentally a word that literally means an easy or a gentle death – or physician-assisted suicide (PAS), given to help the dying across the final threshold, is illegal in this country. In 2001 and 2002, Diane Pretty, suffering from motor neurone disease, took her case to the European Court of Human Rights. She wanted an undertaking that her husband would not be prosecuted if he

helped her die. She lost. In 2002, Reginald Crew, aged seventy-four, who had the same illness, travelled to Switzerland where the organization Dignitas arranged his assisted suicide. Clearly some British citizens are not getting what they want in the way of their own death. The BMA refers to this as 'suicide tourism'. Its weighty tome of medical ethics explains how this has all come about and why the doctors and the lawyers have us hanging on to life beyond what might have been a merciful release. There is much discussion in its pages of 'a good death'. Yet we know that in the real world there are many versions of what that might be: witness Dylan Thomas and John Donne.

Now there are voices from another quarter. A recent survey in the *Nursing Times* finds that one in two nurses does not think it is unethical to administer a lethal injection at a patient's request. As many as 31 per cent said they should be allowed to assist in a patient's death. These are the very people who preside longest and most sympathetically at the bedside of the dying. Clearly the thinking about euthanasia is shifting and public opinion seems to be ahead. Some 82 per cent of the British population think we should each have the right to ask a doctor to end a life afflicted by an incurable and painful disease. The same goes for many countries in Europe. And the nurses go further. Some 40 per cent felt that euthanasia need not apply only in terminal cases, when the assistance is given in the very last hours, but should also be permitted for patients in 'extreme pain or distress'.

How are we to know until we get there what we will want of death? It seems that some patients hoard medicines against the day, hoping that when the doctors refuse, they'll have the means to make their own choice. Yet apparently many who do that in fact don't use them. Every one of us will have our own expectations.

And not only do we not know what others might want; we ourselves in full health or early decline cannot imagine how we will feel further down the line. Once it was for the Church to decide and to preside over our going. Now it's the law and medicine. Surely some greater heed must be paid to the often simple wisdom of ordinary people.

~

IN 2005, IT WAS TIME TO talk again of last things. There were then two poignant photographs in the news. One was of Leslie Burke at the age of forty-five, suffering from cerebellar ataxia and already in a wheelchair, who had just won a judicial review of his case. The other picture was that of Abigail Witchells, paralysed in a hospital bed but smiling at her baby son who, in the arms of his father, was reaching out to her. One was of someone seeking to have control over his own impending death; the other of someone slowly growing back to the life so brutally threatened by a criminal attack on her and her child. What is at question in both is the power of speech. How do we communicate with the world when we can't use words?

Unless we are run over or jump from a bridge, it's likely that towards our final hours or even days we will lose the power of speech. I have sat at the bedside of the dying and I know the problems at first-hand. How are thoughts and wishes to be conveyed? You feel suddenly helpless to know what people want. Imagine how they must feel, with a brain fully active and striving to make contact but slowly drifting away for ever, and at the mercy of others to decide things for them. It is at that moment you wish you had talked things through earlier. That is what Leslie Burke is presently trying to do, and about something quite specific. He wants it made clear that whenever he is 'no longer competent' the doctors will not have the right to deny him food and water because he is saying now that he doesn't want them to be able to do so.

He is right to get things sorted out before it's too late. I have sat beside someone I loved and seen how the failing breath dries out the mouth and leaves the tongue parched. I have helped with regular sponging, to make it possible for the person to gasp a few words. I have watched nurses hold a patient's hand and insistently ask them to 'squeeze once for yes and twice for no'. The dying of the light brings the inevitable fading of the voice. We need to be ready for its going. The problem is that no one wants to talk about it. Death? Leave that till later! I broached the subject with my family once and was kindly reassured that we could get round to that when the time came. But surely it might by then be almost too late. If we want some say in our own deaths we need to speak up now, or we risk being starved to death.

The arguments are already in the courts, which means it's virtually too late. People we don't know are already discussing what might or might not be 'in the patient's best interest'. The British Medical Council, speaking for the doctors, is arguing that a patient does not have the right to insist on any particular form of treatment. A landmark ruling made in Leslie Burke's favour means that doctors must provide treatment – ANH or artificial nutrition and hydration – even though the doctor believes 'the treatment will provide the patient with no clinical benefit or will be futile'. Is keeping someone artificially alive a clinical benefit or not? And is it our right? If so, it's not a very appealing one.

Medical ethics are in a tangle. If it is a doctor's duty to persist in keeping us alive when we have a serious heart attack, massive injuries or untreatable cancer, then it is surely their duty, having landed us in this state, to give us an acceptable death. How do we know what the withdrawal of nourishment feels like? Sadly the situation is unique because the patient can't tick the boxes. The dead don't come back to tell us how bad a long and lingering starvation was compared with an extra shot of morphine or perhaps a mercy-killing pillow. Even those conjured up in a darkened room by mediums usually confine their remarks to comments about the new wallpaper or sending their love to Auntie Flo. If only one of them would say: 'Look, taking away that food and water was really agony. For heaven's sake, when it's her turn, give Auntie Flo a shot of something lethal. Cutting off food and water is a medical cop-out.' Then we might have something to go on. It would almost be worth believing in spiritualism.

~

HOW DO YOU WANT TO be disposed of when you go? Would you like to be shunted into the family vault, I wonder, scion of a long, illustrious line? I remember the late George Howard – he of Castle Howard – showing me rather spookily the exact spot in the family's magnificent mausoleum where his coffin would lie. Most of us don't have such an option. At best, we can ask that those we leave behind open some overgrown grave whose headstone attests to our family membership, but would we expect our survivors to go delving in dusty archives for long-forgotten records? I doubt it. That leaves the option of a new grave or headstone. I have long fancied lying at peace in some idyllic English country churchyard, the wild flowers blowing above me and the needy worms turning me to dust. But that's not a serious option any more, unless you've family connections or pull with the ecclesiastical authorities. English parish churchyards – the Rupert Brooke kind, all daisies and cow parsley – are pretty much full and don't countenance outsiders nudging in on scarce space.

In an overcrowded world we are having to invent new ways of being laid to rest. Far from being a nuisance, the situation is opening up all sorts of new and satisfying opportunities, choices that can often help in the business of bereavement. Most of them focus on the disposal of ashes, which can become something of a consoling ritual. My sister's ashes are scattered round a favourite tree in the garden of her home; I have a friend whose ashes are scattered in the Caribbean in the warm waters of her favourite swim. It's typical of our highly individual age that we don't settle for accepted norms even in death and can even have our say before we go.

But without an actual burial place, how do we want to be remembered? Won't the ashes carry our identities away on the wind or water? For the illustrious dead, of course, statues were the thing, images in stone or bronze of their living presence. The Tudor bishops of Exeter lie virtually end to end in their magnificent cathedral, in the same coloured robes, the same full white sleeves, the same long gowns, as though the existing order would last for ever. In Queen Victoria's heyday, generals and statesmen came to dominate London's plinths. Women, absent from most historic statuary, creep in late with Edith Cavell, Florence Nightingale and Emmeline Pankhurst. It's interesting that the latter monument was raised to arguably the most strident among the suffragettes while the less militant Millicent Fawcett has a mere plaque inside Westminster Abbey. Her husband Henry Fawcett gets the statue. More recently, there was a distinct frisson of disquiet when the statue of Alison Lapper by Marc Quinn was chosen to occupy the empty plinth in Trafalgar Square. In my view it was a rare and impressive tribute.

Today we don't go much for representational statues, perhaps because recent efforts don't have much merit. Anticipating their place in history, sculptures of Mrs Thatcher and Nelson Mandela already exist but they are of such numbing banality as to discourage further such commissions. Perhaps that's why the Diana Memorial has no image of that most image-conscious woman. Safer, they thought, to stay with running water. Mistakenly, as it proved.

Even abstract memorials can bring trouble and it rumbles on. Not long ago a fine sculpture by Maggi Hambling was presented to the Borough of Aldeburgh. It was conceived and made as a tribute to Benjamin Britten, though in no way any kind of likeness. It is a towering sequence of steel seashells interlocking and spreading their fanlike shapes across the shingle. And that's the problem. The siting of the statue divided local opinion, often passionately so. Meetings were called, letters exchanged, voices raised. Like all politicians in a tight spot the local councillor talked resolutely of 'moving on'. But the issue wouldn't die. There was even talk of calling in an ombudsman. Meanwhile Benjamin Britten, celebrated in his music and in the legacy of the Aldeburgh Festival, somehow transcends the squabble.

Even in the grandest places, funerary statuary seems in decline. In Highgate Cemetery, home to the most eclectic and impressive monuments, the famous full-size stone piano (no one ever remembers whom it commemorates) has been vandalized. Highgate, however, still boasts a tribute to Frederick Lillywhite, inventor of cricket's overarm bowling, made up of a bowled wicket in stone with bales flying. In Mortlake's St Mary's Church, there's a full-sized tent to immortalize the explorer Sir Richard Burton. The Victorians treated death as an imperial occasion. We treat it with a more circumspect regard, preferring a cautious ambiguity towards its inexplicable mystery. I'm happy with that. I prefer taking my chances in the elements – loosed on the wind, the sea, the earth – rather than marshalled among the serried ranks of bland stone that offer such unimaginative memorials in today's graveyards.

Epilogue

I WAS BORN INTO A world haunted by two things: the massive
unemployment and depression of the 1930s, and the remorseless
rise of Hitler to power. Society at that time was conventional,
class-bound and elitist. The Church set the moral tone, and
marriage, birth and death were blessed by its sacraments. As a
growing child I lived through the war, a time of fear as well as the
source of an inspiring sense of national purpose. I grew to
maturity in the post-war years when optimism and idealism
blossomed and old patterns began to break up. I saw and rejoiced
at the growth of the welfare state with, for the first time, free
health, free grammar school education, National Insurance,
pensions and industries taken into state ownership on behalf of

the people. Soon just one company ran all the railways – British Rail! Within decades it was mocked and dismantled. Today it seems again like a good idea.

I saw Britain give up its vast empire – the pink parts on the world map – to independence and at the same time experienced the Cold War as a permanent threat. The nuclear danger hovered over my generation, so we marched and protested about that as well as about many other things. In material terms life was getting easier. We began to travel to Europe and to America – glittering across the Atlantic – to share their ideas and cultures. The 1960s brought in a swathe of humane legislation that brought an end to capital punishment, censorship and the criminalization of homosexuality. Divorce and abortion were allowed. The pill was invented and feminism flourished. The 1960s was a liberating decade, freeing us from old and tired conventions and allowing us guilt-free pleasures. We smiled and thrived. So did the country: affluence replaced destitution as more and more people led comfortable lives. By the 1990s the people of Britain were more and more ethnically mixed; a broad range of colours and races characterized our towns and cities. There were and still are tensions, but ways are being found to deal with them. As a pragmatic people we develop solutions as we go along.

But I have lived to see the decline of manners, the widening gap between rich and poor, a rocketing prison population and climbing divorce and abortion statistics. Above all, since the 1990s I have lived to see the triumph of individualism over the common interest. People now live and judge what is best for themselves alone, clinging to their rights as the only way to sustain their place in an increasingly competitive and heartless world. I have watched altruism and a care for the good of all give way to the power of money to define our values and our self-regard. I don't like what I see.

And yet we live in an overwhelmingly congenial culture, a place where music and creativity, food and fashion, holidays and pleasures attend on every hand. The lot of everyone is almost certainly better than it was as I first knew it. Medicine, technology, science: all are fully engaged in a matter we call progress. Is it inevitable that the old in any generation will always complain about the passing of ways of life that seemed good to them? Or has my generation, blessed by an accident of history, actually lived through a golden age of tolerance, concern for society as a whole and enlightenment? I think the latter. What's more, I think there is a sense that the reign of self-interest and the influence of wealth has gone far enough and that other values are re-emerging to claim their place in the human comedy: our common humanity, benevolence, neighbourliness and understanding. I shall live out my life believing this to be true.

Acknowledgements

I owe thanks to the *Guardian* newspaper for allowing me to launch a column in their pages, soon after my seventieth birthday. The delight I took in writing that column, addressing both issues of old age and the very people who were sharing it with me, has led to this book. So my personal thanks go to Lisa Darnell, publisher, Guardian and Observer Books, who so enthusiastically embraced the idea of publication. At Atlantic Publishers I owe much to the support of Alice Hunt and the lively and intelligent collaboration of my editor Louisa Joyner.